TALL STORY

Suggested by *The Homecoming Game* by HOWARD NEMEROV

TALL STORY

A Comedy in Three Acts
by
HOWARD LINDSAY & RUSSEL CROUSE

RANDOM HOUSE, NEW YORK

To
HERMAN SHUMLIN

© COPYRIGHT, AS AN UNPUBLISHED WORK, 1958, BY
HOWARD LINDSAY AND RUSSEL CROUSE

© COPYRIGHT, 1959, BY HOWARD LINDSAY AND RUSSEL CROUSE

All rights, including the right of reproduction in whole or in part, in any form, are reserved under International and Pan-American Copyright Conventions. Published in New York by Random House, Inc., and simultaneously in Toronto, Canada, by Random House of Canada, Limited.

CAUTION: TALL STORY *is the sole property of the producer and the authors, and is fully protected by copyright. It may not be acted, either by professionals or amateurs, without the payment of a royalty. Public readings and radio broadcasting are likewise forbidden. All inquiries concerning rights should be addressed to the authors, Howard Lindsay and Russel Crouse, 13 East 94th Street, New York 28, N.Y.*

The non-professional acting rights of TALL STORY *are controlled exclusively by the Dramatists' Play Service, 14 East 38th Street, New York City, without whose permission in writing no performance of it may be made.*

Photographs by courtesy of Eileen Darby-Graphic House

Manufactured in the United States of America

TALL STORY *was first presented by Emmett Rogers and Robert Weiner at the Belasco Theatre, New York City, on January 29, 1959, with the following cast:*

(*In order in which they speak*)

HERB	Jeff Harris
CONNIE	Nancy Baker
NANCY	Joyce Bulifant
AGNES	Sally Jessup
MARY	Sherry LaFollette
LEON SOLOMON	Hans Conried
CHARLES OSMAN	Marc Connelly
MYRA SOLOMON	Marian Winters
EDDIE	Kevin Carpenter
JOE	Donald Dawson
WALTER	Wayne Tippit
HAZEL	Janet Fox
DON	Bob Lynn, Jr.
WESLEY DAVIS	Jamie Smith
SANDY HARDY	Mason Adams
JUNE RYDER	Nina Wilcox
RAY BLENT	Robert Elston
MIKE GIARDINERI	Ralph Stantley
BAKER	Tom Williams
GRANT	Charles K. Robinson, Jr.
FRED JENSEN	Hazen Gifford
FRIEDA JENSEN	Patricia Finch
DICK STEVENS	Edmund Williams
ALBERT SOLOMON	Ray Merritt
MYERS	Donald Dawson
SIMPSON	Kevin Carpenter
WRIGHT	Wayne Tippit
WYMAN	Jeff Harris
HARMON NAGEL	Robert Wright
COLLINS	John Astin
CLARK	Rex Everhart

Directed by Herman Shumlin

Sets and lighting by George Jenkins

Costumes by Noel Taylor

Incidental songs by Joe Hornsby, Ben G. Allen and Jerry Teifer
(*Arranged by* Edward Thomas)

DRAMATIS PERSONÆ

PROFESSOR CHARLES OSMAN *of the science department. He is a superior person—an individual, without being an eccentric. He is an amused observer of life around him.*

LEON SOLOMON, *assistant professor of ethics. A younger man than Osman, although the father of six children. Solomon is also superior in his own way—probably tall and thin, academic in appearance, capable of suffering and capable of enjoying his suffering. Jewish, but with no accent.*

MYRA SOLOMON (*Leon's wife*), *the mother of his children, the sharer of the self-imposed martyrdoms of her difficult husband because she knows and loves him. Jewish, but with no accent.*

ALBERT SOLOMON, *the ten-year-old son of Myra and Leon.*

RAYMOND (RAY) BLENT, *a senior, over six feet tall on the thin side. Ray is not handsome, but is attractive and immediately likable, although something of a screwball. And Ray is still young, with the nice qualities that go with being young. The first time Ray took his nose out of a book he saw June Ryder.*

JUNE RYDER, *a senior. June came to Custer to get a husband and to become an efficient wife. She is a sturdy, businesslike and direct little girl.*

SANDY HARDY, *the athletic coach. Hardy is a good coach, ambitious for Custer and for himself.*

HARMON NAGEL, *president of Custer. President Nagel is fairly young, distinguished, plausible, and an instinctive leader and a manipulator, with the confidence of the successful man.*

PROSECUTING ATTORNEY DAVIS, *a capable man in his late thirties.*

MIKE GIARDINERI, *a successful restaurateur, Italian, hearty, could possibly be mistaken for a gambler.*

HAZEL, *a friendly, maternal waitress.*

DICK STEVENS, *an assistant coach.*

ED COLLINS *and* BILL CLARK, *Chicago plainclothesmen—not too obvious in type.*

There are other members of the basketball team and other college students of both sexes.

SYNOPSIS OF SCENES

The story takes place at Custer College, a medium sized coeducational institution in the Middle West.

Act One

Scene 1. Mike's College Café. A Monday evening in March.
Scene 2. Coach Hardy's office off the gymnasium. Friday afternoon.
Scene 3. Professor Solomon's living room. The same afternoon.

Act Two

Scene 1. Professor Osman's living room. The same afternoon.
Scene 2. Professor Solomon's living room. Later that afternoon.
Scene 3. Professor Osman's living room. Early that evening.

Act Three

Scene 1. President Nagel's office. The same evening.
Scene 2. Coach Hardy's office. Later that evening.
Scene 3. Professor Solomon's living room. After midnight.

ACT ONE

Scene I

At rise: In the dark is heard the sonorous sound of Westminster chimes, followed by the deep, resonant tones of a bell which could come only from the belfry of a college chapel. This bell sounds eight times, but after the third stroke the sound is diminished as we see in the background the lights come on in the windows of buildings perched somewhat on a hill. As the moonlight comes on, it discloses a building with a high tower and a clock in its belfry, also other buildings of American-collegiate architecture, and the kind of trees that are found on the college campus. It being March, some of these trees are without foliage. At the same time other lights are brought up, disclosing a room in MIKE's *College Café. There are two shallow booths with low backs, stage center. These are capable of seating four customers each. Stage left, against the wall, is a small half-booth for two people only. Stage right is a pay telephone booth. There is a passage behind the booths so that customers can come from the main entrance or the bar, which we assume is offstage right, and cross into another room of the restaurant, which is offstage left. In the back wall, up right, there is the opening of the checkroom through which customers can hand or receive their coats and hats. This is angled so the hat-check girl is never too visible. Inset in the left side of the back wall is a juke box. There is a passageway right of the two center booths and the telephone booth right, and another passageway*

TALL STORY

between the center booths and the small booth on the left for the customers to come through to enter or leave the center booths; and, of course, there is room below the center booths to cross the stage.

As the lights come up on the restaurant, we hear the chatter of conversation from the people who are in these three booths, and from NANCY, *who is talking on the telephone.*

HERB *and* CONNIE, *college students, enter from what is an extension of the café left and cross in the passageway behind the booths,* HERB *stopping at the check room to get his coat. They evidently are quarreling or at least Herb is. None of the opening conversation is distinguishable, but we shall report it as a clue to the characters you are about to meet.*

HERB (*Crossing*) Fine thing! I buy you a dinner and you spend the time flirting with some one else!

CONNIE (*Powdering her nose in unconcern*) Uh-huh!
  (*They exit right*)

NANCY (*Into phone*) You call me at the Delta Gamma house as soon as you get in ... I'll be awfully glad to see you again ... Oh, I didn't expect you to invite me to the game. I just wanted to be sure to see you while you were in town ... Well, I've never really been able to get you out of my mind ... That's great. Well, Friday night then—I'm so excited—Good-bye.
  (*In the right center booth are* AGNES, *an intellectual type, and* MARY, *who is rather plain. They converse as follows*)

AGNES I'm just a coward, that's all, just a coward!

MARY I know just how you feel.

TALL STORY

AGNES Why do I go to the game? You know why—if I didn't go, they'd think I was some kind of freak.

MARY I know just how you feel.

AGNES So there I'll be, watching a lot of bare-legged apple-knockers throw a ball around—a childish game if I ever saw one—and do you know what I'll be missing on TV? Beethoven's *Fifth* with Leonard Bernstein conducting.

MARY I know just how you feel.

AGNES Now, mind you—I don't think that's the last word in music—after all, Beethoven is no Shostakovitch. But when he was alive they must have thought he was very modern and I guess he was when he was alive.

MARY You certainly are intellectual, Agnes. Nancy left this table five minutes ago and we haven't said a word about her. *(She glances toward the phone booth)* Look out, she'll be coming back.
  (In the left center booth, seated on its right, is LEON SOLOMON, *an assistant professor whose subject is modern ethical theory. Next to him is his wife,* MYRA SOLOMON, *and in the left side of the booth,* CHARLES OSMAN, *professor of physics. It is the only table with a table cloth—a checkered one—and there are three coffee cups and saucers, which suggests that they have finished their dinner.* MYRA *and* PROFESSOR OSMAN *have highballs. At this table there is the following animated discussion)*

SOLOMON Just a minute, Charles. When it comes to the raising of children I'm not prepared to accept any celibate advice.

TALL STORY

OSMAN   Celibate! Leon, you're making it very difficult for me me to argue that point in front of Myra.

MYRA   Charles has every right to be offended. You should have called him a bachelor.

SOLOMON   Very well. Let us say bachelor.

MYRA   And even that doesn't guarantee that Charlie has no children.

OSMAN   Thank you, Myra—and if I have I hope they show the civilizing effects of careful discipline.

SOLOMON   Charles, I must repeat, you cannot discipline a child into being a civilized person. You cannot establish ethical or moral standards by taking a child's allowance away from him.

MYRA   Leon means if he gets an allowance.

OSMAN   Don't tell me that children are born with moral standards.

SOLOMON   No. But what establishes moral standards is reason. Not discipline, Charles—reason.
   (*In the stage left booth are two young college students whom we know only as* EDDIE *and* JOE. *Each is drinking what might be beer and they are conversing as follows*)

EDDIE   Want another?

JOE   I ought to be going over my notes. I've got to pass that history exam. I don't know one date from another.

TALL STORY

EDDIE There's only three dates to remember—ten sixty-six, fourteen ninety-two and seventeen seventy-six. Look, Peggy's going to call me any minute. I can't sit here alone.

JOE Suppose she doesn't call?

EDDIE O.K. Then we go to the late flick.

JOE If it was *The Ten Commandments* or something historical I'd have an excuse to go—but what's Brigitte Bardot got to do with history?

EDDIE What's she got to do with history? She makes it.

JOE That's not all she makes.

EDDIE Stick around till Peggy calls—we may do some making ourselves.
    (HAZEL, *the waitress, enters and serves three cocktails to the right center booth. She is followed on by two college boys,* DON *and* WALTER. DON *crosses behind the booths and looks into the room offstage;* WALTER *drops down to* HAZEL's *right. At this point the dialogue becomes distinguishable*)

WALTER Hazel, where's our table?

HAZEL It's in the other room.
    (*She points off right*)

DON (*Calling across from left*) Hey! They're over here!

HAZEL And get way back in the corner. You always make too much noise.

TALL STORY

(*They exit left*)

AGNES Hazel, can we have our check?
(NANCY *comes out of the phone booth*)

HAZEL I'll be with you in a minute.
(*She exits right*)

NANCY (*Rejoining her table*) Well, I've finally got a date for the Ashmore game.

MARY You can't go anywhere without a man, can you? Who's taking you?

NANCY This will positively pulverize you—a guy I know at Ashmore.

AGNES (*The intellectual one*) Ashmore! Nancy, they're such conformists!

NANCY They're very male.

AGNES I had one experience with an Ashmore boy—that was enough. He kept talking all the time about being beat. I thought he was really beat. Well, you can imagine how excited I was! I practically threw myself at him! It turned out he was just plain tired.

MARY (*To* NANCY) You must be pretty desperate to date one of those creeps from Ashmore.
   (*The telephone in the booth rings.* HAZEL *enters in time to hear it*)

AGNES She's just got senior panic.

NANCY You're damn right I have. If I graduate without being engaged, my dad's going to think I wasted his money.

TALL STORY

(HAZEL *has answered the phone, holding the tray outside the booth*)

HAZEL (*Calling*) Eddie, you're wanted on the horn.

EDDIE (*Getting up*) Shall I tell Peggy to get you a date?

JOE (*Uncertainly*) We've got exams day after tomorrow.

EDDIE Ah, come on!

JOE Well, find out who's around.

HAZEL Eddie!
(EDDIE *starts for the phone*)

JOE Hey, Eddie—no Zen Buddhists!
(EDDIE *hurries over to the phone.* HAZEL *has put down the receiver. She goes to the girls' table, leaves her change tray with check, and exits*)

SOLOMON (*Continuing an argument*) Charles, you can't accuse me of being casuistic. I am not saying that you are wrong. All I am saying is that I am right.

OSMAN I won't argue with you. But I wish you wouldn't talk like John Stuart Mill.

SOLOMON What's the matter with John Stuart Mill?—a very rational man.

OSMAN Leon, beware the rational man. He can't think straight.

SOLOMON Charles, you amaze me! That's an extraordinary statement—coming from a scientist.

TALL STORY

MYRA   Leon, I hope you enjoy watching Charlie and me drink. You know you love a bourbon.

OSMAN   (*Extending his drink to* SOLOMON)   Take this. We can order another one.

SOLOMON   (*With a gesture*)   No, thank you.

MYRA   (*Offering hers*)   Have some of mine, huh?

SOLOMON   (*Firmly*)   Myra, you know my rule.
(MYRA *shrugs, then addresses* OSMAN)

MYRA   Leon thinks drinking in front of students sets them a bad example.

OSMAN   I used to think so, too. But the students set me a bad example.

SOLOMON   Forgive me, Charles, but with me it's a matter of principle.

MYRA   Charlie, some people collect first editions. Leon—he collects principles.
(*She puts her hand fondly over* SOLOMON's)

SOLOMON   I'd be a fine teacher of ethics, wouldn't I, if I didn't live up to my own personal standards? (*To* OSMAN) Am I wrong, Charles?

OSMAN   (*Chuckling*)   No, Leon, you just make the mistake of thinking a narrow standard is always a high one. Now, to get back to what started all this. You're new here—

SOLOMON   (*Interrupting*)   Don't misunderstand me. I like it here at Custer.

TALL STORY

MYRA Oh, yes, we like it here.

SOLOMON But I've taught in several other colleges. I've a basis of comparison.

EDDIE (*Calling across from the phone booth*) Hey, Joe!
(JOE *hurries across to the phone booth and waits while* EDDIE *continues to talk on the telephone*)

OSMAN Don't think I'm a chauvinist, but you take any co-educational school in the Middle West and I'll bet you Custer has a higher scholastic standing, a better basketball team and a lower incidence of pregnancy.
(EDDIE *opens the door of the telephone booth*)

JOE Any luck? Who's she got?

EDDIE You know Susan Goodyear, don't you?

JOE Fatso? Is that all that's left around the Theta house?

EDDIE Do you want to cram or do you want to go out with Sue?

JOE (*Thoughtfully*) Ah, Sue's not so bad. There's a lot *of* her.

EDDIE I'll set it up. Remember, you drive!

JOE (*Starting back*) Oh, no, bird dog, we toss for the back seat.
(JOE *goes back to his table, puts down some change, picks up some books and his and* EDDIE's *coats*)

EDDIE (*Into telephone*) Peggy—Joe's just crazy about Sue. Meet you at Elm and Washington—the corner. We're starting now.
(*He hangs up and starts out.* JOE *is on his way and passes*

TALL STORY

in back of the professors' table. He manages a serious, worried look)

JOE Good night, Mr. Osman. Good night, Mr. Solomon.

OSMAN Good night, Knowland.

SOLOMON Good night. (*He watches* JOE *off. Then he shakes his head*) That's what I mean. That's a typical example.

OSMAN Typical of what?

SOLOMON Those worried faces. Nothing on their minds but security.

OSMAN I don't blame them for demanding security. But I don't think that's what's on his mind tonight.
(HAZEL *enters right with* WESLEY DAVIS, *a capable man in his late thirties, who is the county prosecuting attorney. He stops to leave his topcoat at the checkroom.* HAZEL *crosses at the back to the table left, picks up the change and the two glasses*)

HAZEL Here you are, Mr. Davis. Is this all right?

DAVIS Fine! Bring two bourbons on the rocks.

HAZEL A double bourbon.
(DAVIS *sits at the left side of the table*)

DAVIS No, two singles. Sandy Hardy is with me. He's casing the bar. Just wants to make sure his basketball stars aren't training on whiskey.

HAZEL Does the coach think I'd let them get away with anything like that before the Ashmore game? I'll knock his block off. (*She moves to behind* SOLOMON's *table*) Anything else?

TALL STORY

MYRA   Not for me.

OSMAN   No, thank you, Hazel.

DAVIS (*To* OSMAN)   Hi, Charlie!
(OSMAN *turns to see who has spoken*)

OSMAN   How are you, Wes?

MYRA   Does he teach here?

OSMAN   No, he's county prosecutor. An old Custer boy.

SOLOMON   I must have left my cigarettes in my overcoat. (*He starts up*) I'll be right back.
(SOLOMON *starts to the passageway between his booth and the table left*)

MYRA   Leon, telephone the house and tell the baby sitter it's time Albert went to bed.

OSMAN (*To* SOLOMON)   Here, I have cigarettes.
(*He holds out his pack*)

SOLOMON   No, thanks. I'll get my own.

OSMAN   You smoke these, don't you?

SOLOMON   Charles, smoking cigarettes is just burning up money. No one should burn up another person's money.
(SOLOMON *goes to the hat-check door, where, after a time, we see him receive his topcoat, look in the pockets, hand it back, and exit right*)

OSMAN (*Chuckling*)   He's wonderful! I don't know what I would have done this year without him.

MYRA I'm glad. Appreciating Leon takes something special.

OSMAN I have great admiration for him.

MYRA Charlie, not from you—please.

OSMAN What do you mean?

MYRA That's all I hear—"Mrs. Solomon, how much I admire your husband." Just once I'd love to hear someone say he's a swell guy. And do you know, Charlie, he is.

OSMAN Leon has to stay at Custer. That's all there is to it. The chair in his department is vacant. I'm going to see what I can do about it.

MYRA Charlie—don't push. Let's just hope we stay here. Two years at the same college would be wonderful. We've been lucky this year. It's March already and Leon isn't defying anybody. He's not standing on his principles. And he hasn't flunked a son or a daughter of a trustee, I've checked all his classes. There aren't any.
  (*The girls in the right booth rise and start out. They have left money on* HAZEL's *change tray*)

AGNES (*To* NANCY) If you feel that way, why did you come to Custer in the first place?

NANCY Everybody told me it was the best matrimonial agency in the Middle West.

MARY Oh, no—that's Ohio Wesleyan. You have to be engaged to get a diploma.

TALL STORY

(*They exit right, just as* HAZEL *enters with* HARDY, *leading the way to the small table left. She has two bourbons on her tray*)

HAZEL Here you are, Coach. (*She indicates the table*) And you don't need to check up on your team in this restaurant. Not while I'm here.

HARDY You get sore at me and you won't get any tickets for the game Friday night. We'll be ready for another bourbon by the time you get back. Hello, Wes!
(HARDY *sits at the table.* HAZEL *serves them the bourbons.* SOLOMON, *lighting a cigarette, enters from the right, crosses below the booths and reaches his table*)

MYRA Has Albert gone to bed?

SOLOMON Albert? (*It comes to him*) Oh, I forgot. Excuse me again, Charles.
(*He hurries to the telephone booth, reaching for a coin as he goes. He finds he has no change and exits right.* HAZEL *crosses to the right booth, picks up her change tray, clears the glasses, wipes off the table, and puts a "Reserved" sign on the table*)

MYRA Albert is at that terrible age!

OSMAN What age?

MYRA (*After a second's thought*) Well, with Albert it's any age, but he happens to be ten now.

OSMAN Where did Leon start teaching?

15

MYRA His first teaching job was at Fostoria Academy. They always let him come back to Fostoria.

OSMAN Fostoria is a very good school.

MYRA Every other year it is. For us it's a sort of home base; so much so, Charlie, that I feel as though all of our children were born abroad. Albert—he was born at Ohio State.

OSMAN He's the oldest?

MYRA Yes. After Albert came Ruth. She was born at the University of North Dakota. Joel, he was born at Grinnell. The next was Debbie. She was born at Oberlin. Then come the twins. They were born at William and Mary. Nothing's happened at Custer yet, but I'd love to stay here so much I'd take a chance.

OSMAN In my long tenure here I've collected twenty-two godchildren. I can use another. (HAZEL *starts to exit right*) Hazel, you can bring me the check.

HAZEL Yes, Mr. Osman.
(*She exits right*)

MYRA Charlie, don't argue with Leon about the check. He invited you here.

OSMAN On an assistant professor's salary he shouldn't have picked this place. It's expensive.

MYRA You bought his lunch last week at the Faculty Club, didn't you?

OSMAN Yes, the seventy-five-cent lunch.

TALL STORY

MYRA I thought he'd have a nervous breakdown before he paid you back.

OSMAN (*Chuckling*) I've never met anybody quite like him.

MYRA Don't look around. Just settle for Leon.
 (HAZEL *enters left, followed by* JUNE RYDER *and* RAY BLENT. *They are students, seniors.* JUNE *is a wholesome, matter-of-fact girl, majoring in home economics, whose ambition is to run a home and a husband. She is in something of a glow, as she has found a prospect in* RAY. *She is carrying several textbooks, and a couple of notebooks.* RAY *is the star of the basketball team.* HAZEL *leads them to the stage right booth*)

HAZEL Here you are. This is the table reserved for Mr. Jensen.

JUNE Oh, this isn't Mr. Jensen.

RAY No, my name's Blent.
 (JUNE *sits in the booth*)

HAZEL I ought to know Ray Blent when I see him. I've watched you shoot enough baskets. I'll be rooting for you Friday night.

RAY (*Sitting down*) Oh, thank you. We'll just sit down here and wait for the Jensens, if you don't mind. (RAY *gets up in some embarrassment*) Is that all right?

HAZEL You can sit anywhere you want. You're a celebrity. (RAY *takes off his topcoat*) It's too bad about the Jensens—we'll miss them. I'll check your coat.
 (*She takes his coat.* RAY *sits down again*)

JUNE What about the Jensens?

TALL STORY

HAZEL They're leaving college—Fred and Frieda both.

JUNE Oh?

HAZEL I'll be right back.
(*She goes to the coat room, hands in* RAY's *coat and gets a check*)

RAY His father had an operation and Fred has to go home and run the business.

JUNE I didn't know you knew the Jensens that well. Is this to say good-bye to them?

RAY It's a little more than that. It's—well, Professor Wiley was quoting today: "Life gives us but moments and unless we seize the moment . . ."
(*He has his right hand up, ready to seize the moment*)

HAZEL (*Putting the check in his hand*) Here's your check!
(*She exits right*)

RAY Well, anyway, this may be one of those moments. I'm all tensed up. I'm going to have a drink.

JUNE Ray, you can't—you're in training!

RAY I've got to do something. Being engaged all this time is getting to be a strain.

JUNE Don't you want to be engaged?

RAY No . . . I mean, not any longer . . . we've got to do something about it.

JUNE Do what?

TALL STORY

RAY Well, what's the next thing people do after they're engaged?

JUNE (*In surprised reproof*) Ray Blent!

RAY —They get married!

JUNE (*Melting*) Ray, we've been through all that. We're not being married until we have some kind of a home.

RAY All right. I'll agree to that.
  (JUNE *stretches her hand out toward him*)

JUNE Ray, you always end up being so sweet.
  (*He takes her hand*)

RAY June, tonight may be important to both of us. I wish Fred Jensen would get here.
  (*He looks right and sees* HAZEL *appear with a tray holding two glasses of water and two bourbons.* RAY *and* JUNE *quickly pull their hands apart*)

HAZEL Don't mind me. Anything above the table's O.K.
  (*She puts down the water*)

RAY (*A man-of-the-world, he picks up the drink card*) We're going to have a drink while we're waiting. (*Scans the card*) Bring us—two Moscow mules.

HAZEL (*Deadpan*) Two Moscow mules.
  (*She goes to the left booth and serves the bourbons*)

RAY (*Sotto voce, to* JUNE) What is a Moscow mule?

JUNE Ginger beer and vodka.

RAY Maybe I shouldn't have ordered anything that Russian. Scientists have to be very careful these days.

TALL STORY

HAZEL (*To* HARDY) Your star center just came in. Why don't you say hello to him?

HARDY Blent here?
(*He rises and starts for Blent's table*)

RAY I'll take a chance. I feel reckless tonight.

HARDY Hello, Ray! How's the champ!

RAY (*Rising*) Feeling fine—just wonderful! Mr. Hardy, this is Miss Ryder.

JUNE Ray, I know Sandy.

RAY Of course!
(HAZEL *joins them, at* HARDY's *left*)

HARDY Hello, June. How's my favorite cheer leader? (*To* HAZEL) Hazel, this is the most important guy in Custer. Give him anything he wants.

HAZEL Yes, Mr. Hardy. (*She crosses to right of* RAY) What was that order again, Mr. Blent?

RAY Two glasses of milk.

JUNE Make mine a chocolate frappe.

RAY And you can bring me some strawberry Jello.
(*He turns and smiles at* HARDY)

HAZEL Coming up.
(HAZEL *leaves*)

HARDY Well, behave yourselves, and have a good time . . . if that's possible.

TALL STORY

(HARDY *returns to his table.* RAY *sits. He and* JUNE *smile at each other ruefully and hold hands again*)

JUNE   I didn't know anybody ate Jello on purpose.
(SOLOMON *enters from right and goes into the phone booth, puts a coin in the phone, and dials*)

DAVIS (*Craning to look at* RAY)   He's not such a big bastard. What makes him so great?

HARDY   He throws all those baskets scientifically. He's got a system. It's a combination of elliptical trajectories, scalene triangles and the ratio of the energy of the throw to the incidence of concussion against the backboard. I made him write it down for me.

DAVIS   I didn't quite follow it.

HARDY   Don't try to. Nobody understands his theory but himself. But, damn it, it works. Friday night he may break the all-time individual scoring record.

DAVIS   Is he majoring in science?

HARDY   Twenty-four hours a day. I don't know what's going on between him and that girl, but if he's making a pass at her I'll bet he's worked it out scientifically.

JUNE   Really?

RAY   And another thing—research has proved—

JUNE   Ray, can you hold it? I have to make a phone call. I signed up for baby sitting tonight—(*She half starts for the telephone, then sees the booth is occupied*) Somebody's in there. It's Mr. Solomon.

TALL STORY

RAY Professor Solomon? I'm awfully glad you took his course. If we hadn't been in his class together I might never have noticed you.

JUNE Why do you suppose I took that course? Just so you *would* notice me. Who wants modern ethical theory?

RAY Oh, I do. I think I can work out a scientific basis for the difference between right and wrong.

JUNE Wouldn't that take the fun out of it?

RAY You don't understand. I'll explain it to you some day.
(SOLOMON *is opening the door of the telephone booth, and trying to disengage himself from a conversation*)

SOLOMON (*Into telephone*) Albert, I said go to bed!

JUNE I can get to the phone now.
(*She gets a coin from her purse*)

SOLOMON (*Into telephone*) Albert, your argument is sheer sophistry. We're on Central time. Even if it is only six o'clock in California, it's eight o'clock here. Go to bed.
(JUNE *reaches the telephone booth as* SOLOMON *slams the receiver down and steps out*)

JUNE Good evening, Mr. Solomon.

SOLOMON Good evening, Miss Ryder.
(*He starts for his table*)

RAY Good evening, Professor Solomon.

SOLOMON Hello, Blent.
(*He looks at* RAY, *then at* JUNE, *and returns to his table.*

TALL STORY

JUNE *has inserted a coin into the phone and she dials a number*)

MYRA   Has Albert gone to bed?

SOLOMON   He's been told to go to bed—at some length. Charles, your prize science student is here—(*He nods toward the right*) Ray Blent.

MYRA   (*Gesturing* RAY's *height above her own head*) Ray Blent?
(MYRA *looks across toward* RAY)

OSMAN   Blent—here? There's an interesting boy, Leon.

MYRA   I'd like to meet him.

OSMAN   He's a sort of juvenile deliquescent.

MYRA   Huh?

OSMAN   He's disorganized. He could be a genius—but he needs a stabilizing agent.

SOLOMON   I think he's found her.

OSMAN   Blent's with a girl?

SOLOMON   June Ryder. She'd make a good wife. She's got a good head on her shoulders.

OSMAN   Blent's going to need a wife with two heads on her shoulders. Well, I'm glad he's found a girl.
(HAZEL *enters with the frappe, the milk and the Jello, and serves them, then exits right.* MIKE *enters from left, sees* HARDY *and slaps him on the shoulder*)

23

TALL STORY

MIKE Hello, Coach! (*He proceeds to* OSMAN's *table*) Mr. Osman, I just heard you were here. Everything all right?

OSMAN Fine.

OSMAN Mike, this is Mr. and Mrs. Solomon.

MIKE How do you do? (*To* OSMAN) What did you have for dinner?

OSMAN Scallopine marsala.

MIKE Was it good?

OSMAN I couldn't have done it better myself.

MIKE (*To the* SOLOMONS) If he ever invites you to dinner at his house, you go. Any time he wants a job as chef I've got one waiting for him. And chefs make more money than professors.

MYRA Everybody makes more money than professors.
    (MIKE *laughs and turns back to the left booth.* HAZEL *enters with the check for* SOLOMON. *She hands it to him from behind the booth, then exits right*)

MIKE Hiya, Coach. (*He sees* DAVIS) Mr. Prosecutor. (*He turns back to* HARDY) All set for the Ashmore game?
    (JUNE *comes out of the telephone booth and returns to her table*)

DAVIS (*Significantly*) What are the odds on the game, Mike?

MIKE (*Innocently*) How do I know? I don't make book. It's against the law. (*To* HARDY) It says in the papers Michigan State is after you.

TALL STORY

HARDY   Don't believe all you see in the papers.

DAVIS   Mike . . .

MIKE   (*To* HARDY)   You wouldn't leave Custer for Michigan State, would you?

HARDY   I love it here.

DAVIS   (*Knowingly*)   Mike, if you did make book, what would the odds be?

MIKE   Oh, I'd lay two to one. I mean it figures two to one, eleven to five—unless somebody breaks a leg.

DAVIS   Is there much action, Mike?

MIKE   (*To* HARDY)   All the boys in good shape?

HARDY   Yeah.

MIKE   How about Blent?

HARDY   Ask him yourself. He's right over there.
   (*He indicates* RAY *with his head*)

MIKE   Ray Blent? In my place? (*Sees* RAY) You're right. Excuse me.
   (*He starts for* RAY's *table, crossing behind the booths*)

HARDY   Mike don't make book.

DAVIS   The hell he doesn't! I'll nail him some day.

MIKE   (*Reaching the right booth*)   Hey, you're Ray Blent!

RAY   Yes, sir.

MIKE I'm Mike—Mike Giardineri.
(*They shake hands*)

RAY How do you do? This is Miss Ryder.

MIKE (*To* JUNE) Hello. (*He turns back to* RAY) Say, you know something—you're great! I watch you play every game. You never eat in my place before. Why not?

RAY I eat at the Co-op. I wait on table there.

MIKE Why? You eat here. I pick up the check.

RAY Thank you very much, but I like to pay my own way.

MIKE Look, you don't lose your amateur standing. This is just honest graft.

RAY Thanks just the same.

MIKE O.K.
(HAZEL *has entered. She taps* MIKE *on the shoulder*)

HAZEL Somebody in your office wants to see you.

MIKE Who is it?

HAZEL Some guy—I don't know him.
(HAZEL *exits right*)

MIKE (*To* RAY) Enjoy yourself. Drop in again.
(MIKE *exits right.* SOLOMON *has put some money on* HAZEL's *change tray*)

OSMAN Leon, at least let me leave the tip.

SOLOMON   That's impossible. You're my guest.
(OSMAN *rises and so does* MYRA)

MYRA   Charlie, would you introduce me to Ray Blent?

OSMAN   Myra, you're just a fool for a pretty face. Come along!

SOLOMON   I'll get the coats.
(MYRA *leads the way to the right table,* OSMAN *following her.* SOLOMON *crosses left, then behind the booths to the checkroom, where he gets his and* OSMAN's *coats*)

OSMAN   Hello, Blent.

RAY (*Rising*)   Good evening, sir. This is Miss Ryder.

OSMAN   Mrs. Solomon, this is Miss Ryder and Ray Blent.

MYRA   Ray Blent! This is a real pleasure.

RAY   It's a pleasure to meet you, Mrs. Solomon. Your husband is a wonderful man.

MYRA (*Beaming*)   Oh, you really think so?

RAY   Yes, I certainly admire him.
(MYRA *looks at* OSMAN, *her beam fading*)

MYRA   Uh-huh!

OSMAN   Uh-huh!

MYRA (*To* RAY *and* JUNE)   Well—good night.
(*She joins* SOLOMON)

RAY   Mr. Osman, that man from Monsanto Chemical—(*Taking a letter from his pocket*) I had another letter from him. Would it be possible for me to talk to you about it?

OSMAN Certainly. Any afternoon. You know I'm always glad to talk to you. Good night.

JUNE Good night, sir.
(OSMAN *joins the* SOLOMONS, *and they all exit right*)

JUNE What's that letter from the chemical company? (*She takes it from* RAY's *hand and unfolds it*) Have you got a job already?

RAY (*Sitting*) I've had offers from five different companies.

JUNE Now I've got something to write my father about! (*She reads the letter eagerly*)

DAVIS Do you want to bet?

HARDY (*Positively*) Hogan was open champion in nineteen fifty-two.

DAVIS Ten dollars says he wasn't.

HARDY (*Very positive*) Hogan was open champion . . . (*He hesitates*) Wait a minute. When I'm this sure I'm right I'm usually wrong.

JUNE This doesn't mention pension plan or group insurance.

RAY Oh, all that stuff was in their first letter.

JUNE This is kinda vague. It doesn't say what salary increase you'll get the third year. We'll have to go into this pretty seriously.

RAY Of course. This is a very serious matter. You see, I'm not sure that's what I want to do.

TALL STORY

JUNE What don't you want to do?

RAY Make money.

JUNE Ray, what did you say?

RAY I said I'm not sure I want to make money.

JUNE What else would you do?

RAY Contribute!

JUNE Contribute?

RAY Yes, like a Schweitzer or a Jonas Salk.

JUNE (*Remembering*) Oh, yes. That's a side of you I always admired, but I didn't know you meant it. Ray, you're a real screwball—I guess that's why I love you. (*She puts the letter in her handbag*) Be sure to tell me about those other offers. Eat your Jello.
    (*At this point,* BAKER, GRANT, NANCY *and* AGNES *enter.* BAKER *is well ahead. They cross behind the booths. Both* GRANT *and* BAKER *carry a glass of beer*)

BAKER Come on, here's a table.
    (*They pass* RAY's *table*)

AGNES Hi, Juney!

GRANT (*Mussing* RAY's *hair*) Hi, shorty.

RAY Hello, Tommy.
    (*The four arrive at the left center booth and sit*)

GRANT What gives here anyway? Ray Blent in Mike's!

TALL STORY

AGNES Don't worry. I looked. He's drinking milk.

GRANT There are other ways a hammerhead can break training.

BAKER He's not going to be led astray by "Miss Deep-Freeze!"

NANCY How do you know she's a Deep-Freeze?

BAKER There's one sure way of finding out—you try.

NANCY Then they're both safe. He's strictly from left field.

FRED (*Off*) Hiya, Hazel! Where's Mike? Out to dinner some place? Ha, ha!
 (*He laughs at his own joke*)

RAY Here they are!

HAZEL (*Off*) First booth, Mr. Jensen.
 (FRED *and* FRIEDA JENSEN *enter from left.* FRED *and* FRIEDA *are both about twenty-four.* FRED *is a personality kid.* FRIEDA *is a wife*)

FRED Where's that big basketball star? He wants to buy me a drink. (*He sees* RAY) Hiya, big boy!
 (RAY *rises and shakes hands with* FRED)

RAY Hello, Fred. Hello, Frieda. Sit down.
 (FRIEDA *sits beside* JUNE, FRED *next to* RAY)

JUNE Frieda, I just heard you've got to leave school! That's terrible! I'm just snowed!

FRIEDA Yes, it's really rugged. Fred has to go to work.

FRED You know what I say? I say *"C'est la vie!"* And that proves I didn't study French for nothing.

RAY I'm glad you're taking it that way. I thought you'd be very depressed.

FRIEDA When he opens that office every morning he'll be depressed.

FRED When I think that Ray Blent, the greatest basketball player in the country, wanted to get together for a farewell drink—say, this means more to me than anything that's happened since I've been in college—and I've been here six years.

FRIEDA Believe it or not, Fred had a good chance of graduating this year.
  (HAZEL *enters, crosses behind the booths, comes down to the left center table and serves cocktails to* NANCY *and* AGNES)

FRED June, ten years from now this guy is going to be the most famous scientist in the world—another Machiavelli. Ha! Ha!
  (*He enjoys this*)

FRIEDA Juney, don't let Ray get away from you.

JUNE Don't worry!

RAY As a matter of fact, that's what I wanted to talk to you about. Fred, I hear you want to sell your trailer?

FRED There's no two ways about it—we've got to sell it.

RAY (*To* FRED) I've got news for you. (*He takes a dramatic pause*) We want to buy it!

JUNE Ray!
(*She kisses him*)

FRIEDA Oh, June!
(FRIEDA *embraces and kisses* JUNE)

FRED (*Shaking* RAY's *hand*) Ray, congratulations! You, too, Juney!

JUNE (*Surprised but happy*) Well, it's the first I've heard of it.

FRED This calls for a drink. Hazel! (HAZEL *is on her way to the right table*) Ray, there's nobody I'd rather sell that trailer to. (HAZEL *arrives at the table*) Hazel, bring us two white mustangs.
(HAZEL *exits right*)

FRED Frieda, this is a great break. (*To* JUNE *and* RAY) I have to leave on the midnight tonight. Frieda was going to wait until she sold the trailer. (*To* FRIEDA) Now you can leave any time.

FRIEDA Not until Friday night after the game.

RAY Well, I'm glad it's all settled. How much do you want for it?

FRED I told Frieda she had to get twelve hundred and fifty dollars—but for Ray Blent we'll practically make it a wedding present—twelve hundred.

RAY Fred, we'll never forget you for this. I'll pay Frieda a hundred and fifty dollars down tomorrow morning.

FRED Fine. And you can get the rest of it to her before she leaves Friday.

TALL STORY

RAY Well, I'm pretty sure I know where I can borrow another fifty dollars.

FRED That leaves a thousand. When are you going to come up with that?

RAY You're going to have to trust me for it.

FRED What's a thousand dollars? Get it from your folks.

RAY I haven't got any folks. You know that.

FRED I mean that uncle of yours.

RAY He just pays my tuition. I couldn't ask him for anything like a thousand dollars. (*There is an embarrassed pause*) Fred, you know I'm good for it. You've always said I had a great future.

FRED Yeah, but who knows when it's going to start? Ray, up to four o'clock this afternoon I was a college student—you know, happy-go-lucky, give you my shirt. Now I'm a businessman—a whole new setup—businessmen want cash.
  (*There is a pause. The telephone rings.* HAZEL *has entered just in time to hear this and she answers the phone*)

JUNE Ray, we don't have to be married right away.

RAY (*Fiercely*) Yes, we do.
  (HAZEL *comes out of the booth and speaks to* RAY)

HAZEL Mr. Blent, you're wanted on the horn.

RAY (*Rising*) Me? Are you sure? Nobody knows I'm *here*.

HAZEL They said Ray Blent.
  (FRED *rises to let* RAY *out of the booth, then sits again*)

33

RAY   Excuse me. Fred, we've got to work this out somehow. I'll be right back.
   (*He goes into the booth.* HAZEL *exits. Both of the girls look at* FRED)

FRIEDA   Fred feels terrible about this—don't you, Fred?
   (*She kicks* FRED *under the table*)

FRED   I should say I do.

RAY (*Into telephone*)   Hello! Hold on just a minute. (*He steps back to* FRED) Fred, it just came to me . . . I can give you my I.O.U. I'll give it to you right here before you go. You just wait. (RAY *returns to the telephone*) Hello!

FRED   June, an I.O.U's no good. I'm leaving some of mine all over campus.

RAY (*Into telephone*)   Who's this?

FRED (*Looking at his watch*)   Frieda, we've got to say goodbye to the Wallaces. (*He rises*)

FRIEDA   Who?

FRED (*Through his teeth*)   The Wallaces. You know I promised we'd drop in.
   (FRIEDA *gets it and rises*)

RAY (*Into telephone*)   Red? Red who?

FRED   Say good-bye to Ray, will you? Come on, Frieda!

FREIDA   See you tomorrow, Juney.

RAY (*Into telephone*)   Well, if I don't know you, what'd you call me for?

TALL STORY

FRED Congratulations to both of you. That was great news. (*They start out. They meet* HAZEL *as she enters with the drinks on her tray.* FRED *stops her with a gesture, takes a drink off the tray.* FRED *and* FRIEDA *exit.* HAZEL *shrugs and follows them off*)

RAY (*Into telephone*) . . . Listen, mister, Ashmore hasn't got a chance . . . I don't follow you . . . Look, Red, whoever you are, I want to get back to my table. What's this all about? . . . Fifteen hundred? Fifteen hundred what? . . . Fifteen hundred dollars? . . . What for? . . . What kind of proposition? . . . Who is this? . . . Listen . . . you're talking to the wrong man! It's a good thing you're not here . . . I'd hit you right in the nose! . . . I don't have to think it over . . . Go to hell!! (*He hangs up. Then he picks up the receiver again*) Hey, you—do you know what I think of you? Hey—Hello?—Damn it! (*He slams the receiver down this time and starts left, behind the booths, toward* HARDY'S *table*) Coach, I just had the damnedest telephone call—(RAY *stops short at his own table, noticing the* JENSENS *are missing. To* JUNE) Where are the Jensens?

JUNE They had to go. They remembered another date.

RAY But we've got to get this thing settled tonight.

JUNE Ray, Fred made it very clear they're not going to sell it except for cash.

RAY All right, the hell with the Jensens—the hell with their trailer. We're going to get married anyway. (*He sits beside* JUNE)

JUNE Of course we're going to get married. But it doesn't have to be right away. Just as soon as—

TALL STORY

RAY Not just as soon as—*Now!*

JUNE Ray, don't flip. We can wait.

RAY I can't wait. The way I feel about you—the way I think about you—you don't know—I can't *wait*.

JUNE You talk as though you wanted to sleep with me!

RAY I do!

JUNE Ray!

RAY That's why we have to get married right away.

JUNE I never thought I'd hear you talk like that.

RAY June, you're a sweet, good girl. I know you're good. I hear the boys talk about you around the campus. That's one of the things that made me fall in love with you. Maybe this is something that only men would understand—but I can't keep certain thoughts out of my head—you don't know how desperate this is.

JUNE Why, darling?

RAY I'm up against something where science can't help me!

JUNE Ray dear, I want to be married just as much as you do. Why do you suppose I majored in home economics?

RAY I'm pretty sure my uncle's going to give me a check when I graduate. I've got a hunch it will be maybe a thousand dollars—I wish I had the nerve to tackle him . . .

JUNE I've got an aunt that's loaded. But if I ever asked her for a nickel my mother would kill me. She's my father's sister.

TALL STORY

(JUNE *looks at her watch*) Do you know what time it is? I'm due to baby sit at President Nagel's in fifteen minutes. I've got to fix my face. Ray, don't look so worried. I love you.
(*She kisses him, gets up and exits left.* GRANT *goes over to the juke box, selects a tune and puts a nickel in. We hear a lively record.* GRANT *returns to his table.* HAZEL *enters and goes to* RAY's *table*)

HAZEL Anything else?

RAY No, thanks. Just the check, please.
(HAZEL *tears off the check and hands it to* RAY *on the change tray. He has a bill in his hand, puts it on the tray and reaches into his pocket*)

HAZEL No tip—just make thirty or forty baskets Friday night.
(HAZEL *takes the change tray and exits left.* RAY *has fished in his pocket and pulled out a coat check. He wanders up to the checkroom, hands it in. A coat is handed out by an invisible check girl. He puts down a tip and goes back to his table, putting his topcoat on. He stands looking off for* JUNE. *Absent-mindedly, he puts his hand into his topcoat pocket, looks a little surprised and puzzled, and pulls out a long Manila envelope from his pocket, raises the flap and looks inside and is startled. He crams the envelope back in his pocket, looks toward the telephone, then quickly sits down. He takes the envelope out again furtively, reaches inside it and takes out a large stack of bills and fans them. He puts them back in the envelope quickly, and sits, frozen.* HAZEL *enters left and puts a check on the left table.* HARDY *puts down a couple of bills*)

HARDY Here you are, Hazel.

TALL STORY

HAZEL Thanks.
(HAZEL *exits right.* HARDY *and* DAVIS *rise and start out. As they reach* RAY, HARDY *stops*)

HARDY Ray!
(RAY *jumps up, and holds his hands out to receive a basketball which he apparently expects to receive from any direction*)

RAY Yes, sir! Yes, sir.

HARDY I want you to meet Mr. Davis. This is Mr. Blent.
(DAVIS *reaches out to shake hands*)

RAY How are you, Mr. Blent? Oh, no! I'm Blent.

DAVIS Yes, and I think you're pretty wonderful.

RAY Yes, I am. I mean—

DAVIS I'll be there Friday night.

RAY Friday night?
(*He looks at the coach for a clue*)

HARDY The game.

RAY Oh, yes, the game. I expect to be there, too.
(HARDY *looks at* RAY, *puzzled*)

HARDY Come on, Wes.
(*They exit.* RAY *sits down again.* JUNE *comes back to the table from the powder room and begins to collect her books. The music of the record finishes.* GRANT *goes to the juke box and again studies the selections*)

TALL STORY

JUNE Are you ready?

RAY Oh! Yes. Sure.
(*He gets up slowly*)

JUNE Going to the library?

RAY No, I think I'll just walk around for a while. June, if we could have bought the trailer, would you have married me right away?

JUNE (*After a moment's thought*) Yes—I would. You see, a trailer's a home we could take with us anywhere. It might come in handy in Texas.

RAY Texas? What are we doing in Texas?

JUNE (*Now ready to leave*) I've been thinking—that letter from those chemical people—that came from Texas—their plant is down there. If you took that job we could maybe live in the trailer until we could buy a ranch house. Come on!
(*She goes out.* GRANT *drops a coin in the juke box. A noisy rock-'n' roll record starts.* RAY *stands for a moment trying to adjust himself to a new plan of life, then follows* JUNE *off*)

The Lights Fade Out

Scene 2

The office of COACH HARDY. *The following Friday afternoon. The office is off the gymnasium and close enough to the basketball floor so that when the doors to the main hall are open we can hear the cheers of the crowd when a game is being played, or the voices of the cheer leaders when they are practicing. There is a door down right to the coach's inner office. The left side wall has a single door to the outside, extreme down left. In the center upper left wall are double swinging doors leading to the corridor and the gymnasium. The walls are covered with photographs of former teams. There is a cabinet upper right center containing trophies, cups, etc., and there is a steel locker up center. There is a desk with telephone right center, with a chair behind it and a single chair left of the desk. There is a flat bench, about six feet long, above the door down right, parallel with the footlights, and a short bench below the door down left.*

At rise: The stage is empty. STEVENS, *the assistant coach, dressed in slacks and a T shirt, carrying a basketball, enters through one of the double doors upper left center. He pauses in the doorway, listening to part of a college cheer done by about six voices—the cheer leaders practicing. Up to the time the team comes onstage, whenever the doors to the corridor are opened we hear part of a college cheer.* STEVENS *crosses down right. As the door up left center closes, the sound of the cheer stops. He opens the door down right and calls through it.*

STEVENS   O.K., Sandy. I'm back.

HARDY (*Off*)   Did you get ahold of Blent?

STEVENS Yeah! Blent will be up as soon as he's changed. I told the others to stay in the locker room until you send for them.

HARDY (*Off*) Wait a minute. I've got something for you to do. (STEVENS *goes to the desk and puts the basketball down on it so that he can light a cigarette.* HARDY *comes on, carrying an old shoe box under one arm and a book in the other hand, with his finger marking a place. He puts the book on the desk, spreading it open at the marked place. He takes a bundle of tickets with a rubber band around them out of the shoe box and hands them to* STEVENS) Take these tickets over to the dean's office. The faculty's going to raise hell about the locations, but it's the best I could do.

STEVENS I'll just drop them and run.

HARDY I'd love to work in a college where there wasn't any faculty. They waste so much time around here on education. No wonder this generation is mixed up.
    (HARDY *sits at the desk.* STEVENS *picks up the book and reads the title*)

STEVENS *Plane and Solid Geometry.* What the hell are you doing with this?

HARDY I was trying to figure out some way to talk to Blent in his own language.

STEVENS Sandy, don't you worry about Blent. He'll come through tonight.

HARDY He's way off his game. I've gotta try to find out why.

STEVENS (*Indicating the book*) Do you think this will help?
    (HARDY *takes the book from* STEVENS)

TALL STORY

HARDY I don't know. It's pretty deep stuff. Did you know that a square is a rectangle but a rectangle isn't always a square?

STEVENS That sounds like jive talk.

HARDY No, I figured it out. O.K. So what did it get me?

STEVENS (*Going to the corridor door*) You worry too much. (*He opens the door. We hear part of a cheer*) Oh—are you going to use the floor or is it all right for the cheer leaders to go on practicing there?

HARDY Let them go ahead. I'm just going to have a little skull practice in here. (STEVENS *starts out, stops as* HARDY *speaks*) Steve, do you suppose it's girl trouble? Blent was in Mike's with that cheer leader—you know, Ryder—Monday night. He made less sense than usual.

STEVENS I thought of that angle. I checked on her. Everybody says she's a nice, level-headed kid. She's not the kind that would—
  (RAY *steps into the room. He has, however, left his mind somewhere outside. Again while the doors are open we hear a part of the offstage cheer*)

STEVENS Hi, Ray! Sandy, here's Blent!
  (STEVENS *exits.* HARDY, *who appeared worried before, takes on a hearty and brisk manner*)

HARDY Come in, Ray—come in! How's the boy? Glad to see you, fella. You're looking great—just great! (*Not too sure about this after looking at* RAY) You feel all right?

Nina Wilcox, Robert Elston and Ray Merritt
as JUNE RYDER, RAY BLENT and ALBERT SOLOMON

TALL STORY

RAY June, this isn't the time to talk about that.

JUNE I've got to talk about it.

RAY Well, if you're going to stay here, you go out and put some clothes on.

JUNE Frieda's half crazy. I told her yesterday we were going to buy the trailer. I told her your uncle had come through with the money.

RAY June, we shouldn't be here alone together in our bare legs. We'll talk about it after the game.
  (RAY *dribbles the ball all over the office, and* JUNE *follows him about. Occasionally he tosses the ball over her head and catches it on the other side of her*)

JUNE It can't wait until after the game. Frieda's got a roomette on the midnight. Fred's meeting her in Omaha. She can't go until she gets the money. You were supposed to give it to her at English lit this morning. And you cut English lit ... And you didn't meet me at the Co-op for lunch—for the first time since we've been engaged! (*He goes on dribbling*) Ray, have you changed your mind? (*Then, forlornly*) Have you changed your mind about marrying me?
  (RAY *stops short, holding the ball*)

RAY Oh, honey, don't ever say that!

JUNE (*Half crying*) What am I going to think?

RAY You know I want to marry you. Don't ever say that!

JUNE (*Exasperated*) Then why didn't you pay Frieda for the trailer?

TALL STORY

RAY June, we can't buy the trailer with that money.

JUNE Why not?

RAY Our first home—I think we ought to buy it with money I've worked for—I mean, money I've earned myself . . . honestly.

JUNE This puts me in a hell of a spot with Frieda. I don't dare ask my aunt for anything. Ray, just tell me why—

RAY (*Sharply*) We're not going to use that money!
(*She stares at him, surprised at his tone*)

JUNE Why not? What's the matter with your uncle's money?
(*He dribbles left*)

RAY There's plenty the matter with it.
(JUNE *follows him. He fakes a shot, then dashes behind her, to center*)

JUNE Ray, you showed it to me. It's perfectly good money, isn't it?

RAY No—I mean, yes—I mean it's good in the sense that it's money—but it isn't money I can use in the sense that it's good.

JUNE Ray—you sound confused.

RAY I *am* confused. That's one thing I'm very clear about.
(*He dribbles left again, and poses for a "free throw"*)

JUNE All right—but there's something *I* want to be clear about.
(*At this point* HARDY *enters just as* JUNE, *by a swift*

maneuver, takes the ball away from RAY. RAY, *tense and drawn, sits on the bench down left*)

HARDY Good work, Ryder! I may have you in there tonight. (JUNE *starts for the door, carrying the ball*) How good are you at putting that ball in a basket? (JUNE *rams the ball into* HARDY's *midriff, knocking the wind out of him. She stalks out.* HARDY *looks at* RAY) Well, did you get everything straightened out? (*A group of basketball players*—GRANT, BAKER, MYERS, SIMPSON, WRIGHT *and* WYMAN, *in uniform, enter, chattering noisily. They grab the ball from* HARDY *and start tossing it around*) Wait a minute! I've got some good news. I snagged some more seats for you. (*There are expressions of delight*) I've got one lousy pair for each of you . . . (*Groans*) . . . One pretty good pair—and one pair of honeys. They're in the faculty section. Come and get 'em.

(*He reaches into the shoe box and tosses a bundle of tickets on the table. All the boys, except* RAY, *spring forward with a great deal of chatter. The ad libs mount to quite a din. Suddenly the door is thrown open and an excited* STEVENS *enters*)

STEVENS Hey, fellows! Sandy! Fellows! Ray!

HARDY What's the matter?
(*The others continue talking noisily, except* RAY, *who sits silent.* STEVENS *blows a shrill blast on his whistle. Everything stops short. There is a tense silence.* STEVENS *walks straight to* RAY)

STEVENS Ray, how could you do this to us?

RAY What?

TALL STORY

STEVENS Everybody thought you were so wonderful!

HARDY What is this?

BAKER What's up?

GRANT What's he done?

HARDY Steve, what the hell's happened?

STEVENS What's happened? He flunked in physics!

BAKER You're kidding, Steve.

GRANT Don't give us that.

STEVENS It's just been posted!

RAY Flunked!

    (*The boys have crowded around* RAY)

BAKER (*To* STEVENS) Are you positive?

STEVENS Go look for yourself.

BAKER You mean he can't play tonight?

GRANT He's ineligible?

STEVENS You know the rules.

RAY I can't play.

HARDY They can't do this to me—they just can't do this to me. Who flunked him?

STEVENS Osman!

GRANT Charlie Osman?

TALL STORY

STEVENS (*To* RAY) How could you flunk an exam in physics?

BAKER Blent, get over to Osman's right away and talk to him.

HARDY (*Taking over*) Wait a minute! (*Concentrating a moment*) Ray, you stay here. The rest of you boys go over and talk to Osman. Give him the works. Ride him like you would a forward. Tell him he can't do this to Custer. Keep right on him—don't let up until he says Ray can play.
(*The boys rush out.* HARDY *goes to the telephone and starts dialing*)

STEVENS Aren't you going with 'em, Sandy?

HARDY No, I'm going to shoot from another angle. You get 'em started. (STEVENS *exits*) Ray boy, we're not licked yet. You know what General Custer said—"Don't give up the ship!" (*Into telephone*) Hello, Miss Federman . . . This is Sandy Hardy . . . I have to speak to President Nagel . . . How soon will he be free? . . . It's about Osman flunking Ray Blent . . . I just want to talk to him . . . to tell him to get to work on it right away . . . What! . . . What other course? . . . Modern ethical theory? . . . Is that something they study around here? . . . Who teaches such a thing? . . . SOLOMON! Oh, my God! Then I've got to interrupt him. I'm coming over. I'm on my way . . . and I'm warning you, if you try to run interference, I'll go right around your end!
(JUNE *enters, still in cheer-leader's costume.* HARDY *hangs up, and gets his overcoat out of the locker.* JUNE *goes to* RAY)

JUNE Ray, is it true?
(RAY *rises and crosses to right center*)

49

TALL STORY

HARDY (*To* RAY) How stupid can you get? You flunked two exams! With the Conference championship riding on this game! All that it meant to you—all that it meant to the team—(*He starts for the door*) and all that it meant to Custer. (*At the door*) And this may cost me that job at Michigan State.

(*He exits.* RAY *has sunk onto his haunches, a picture of dejection. He is staring at the floor.* JUNE *goes to him*)

JUNE I just can't believe it. What happened, Ray? Ray, what happened? (*He does not look at her*) Look at me, Ray! Look at me!

(RAY *turns his head and looks. In front of his eyes are* JUNE's *bare legs. With a groan he stretches out full-length on the floor*)

The Lights Black Out

Scene 3

The living room of LEON SOLOMON's *home. The same afternoon. The room has the look of a house rented for temporary occupancy. There is a window in the right wall. Above this, on an angle, is the door to the porch. When this is open, we can see a trellis with perhaps some ivy. In the upper wall, left of the front door, are a few steps, with a short stair rail, which suggest a flight of stairs that lead to the upper floor. The center wall cuts off the view of the rest of the stairs. On it hang some shelves, which serve as a bookcase, and a few pictures. The left wall contains the swinging door leading to the kitchen. Below this door, against the left wall, is a modern bucket chair. Across the left center of the room is a sofa with an end table at its right. There is a low lamp on the end table. On a narrow table behind the sofa is the telephone and a pencil and long strip of paper on which is a list of names. Down right, against the right wall, is a baby's play pen. Over its sides are hung some children's clothes. Clothes are also thrown carelessly on the sofa and in the chair down left. The back wall above the stairs is adorned by finger paintings and juvenile water colors. At the foot of the stairs, in front of the stair rail, is a clothes tree. There is a stool down right center.*

At rise: MYRA SOLOMON *is behind the sofa, with the telephone receiver to her ear.*

MYRA (*Into phone*)   Mr. Solomon hasn't come home yet. (*Pistol shots from a toy pistol are heard offstage*) He should be back any minute. (*Shots are heard again; both pistol and toy*

TALL STORY

machine gun) Please hold on. (*She puts down the phone and goes to the door*) Albert! Albert, get up off that grass! (*There is a pause*) Albert, did you hear me? (*She closes the door and returns to the phone*) Hello . . . What name shall I say? Oh. You called before, didn't you? (*She lifts from the table a piece of paper with a long list of names, and consults it*) Yes, your name is ninth on the list . . . He'll call you . . . Thank you. (*She hangs up and studies the list. She shows some wonder but is rather pleased. We hear again the toy machine gun offstage. She puts down the list and hurries to the door and calls out*) Albert, I told you to get up off the grass. (*We hear a child's voice off*) I don't care if you have been killed. You can be dead standing up. (*The telephone rings again*) Albert, you get up or I'll tell your father. And you know what he'll do! (*The telephone continues ringing. She hurries back to it, speaking to herself*) He'll reason with you. (*Into telephone*) Hello . . . Mr. Solomon hasn't come home yet . . . Have you called before? . . . Who shall I say? (*She writes down a name, then a number*) 1-3-4-7—I've got it . . . Thank you. (*She hangs up and with her pencil begins to count the number of names. The telephone rings again. Into telephone*) Hello . . . Mr. Solomon hasn't come home yet . . . who is this? . . . (*Impressed*) The president of the Student Council . . . I'll have him call you first . . As soon as he comes in . . . Thank you. (*As she is hanging up,* SOLOMON *enters, bringing* ALBERT *in with him, with a tight grip on his arm.* SOLOMON *is wearing a topcoat*) Leon, why are you so late?

(SOLOMON *realizes attack is the best defense*)

SOLOMON Myra, why it is every time I come home Albert is lying on the grass?

TALL STORY

(He releases ALBERT *and hangs up his coat)*

MYRA   Albert, I warned you. Where have you been, Leon?

SOLOMON   I've been at the Faculty Club, an organization composed entirely of gentlemen who have lost their faculties.
(He crosses to down left)

MYRA   What happened? You can tell me later. You've become very popular.

SOLOMON *(Ironically)*   Popular?

MYRA   You've had all these phone calls.
(She holds out the list)

SOLOMON   That can wait, Myra. Albert!

MYRA   All these people are waiting. I told them you'd call them right away.

SOLOMON   Albert, come here! (ALBERT *goes to his father*) Do you remember our last conversation on the subject of dignified behavior? Do you remember what I said?

ALBERT   Do you remember what *I* said?

SOLOMON   Albert, don't argue with me. I'm in no mood for it.

ALBERT   Father, you're not treating me like a person.

SOLOMON   As a person!

ALBERT   As a person.
(He retreats to his mother, who puts her hand on his forehead)

SOLOMON   Albert, the correct use of English is the mark of an educated man. (*He turns away*) Although there are those who think throwing a ball into a basket is a triumph of education.

MYRA   Albert, go get the thermometer. You may have a temperature.

ALBERT (*At the foot of the stairs*)   Mother, the human animal always has a temperature. What you mean is I may have a fever.

SOLOMON   Go get the thermometer! (ALBERT *hurries upstairs.* SOLOMON *crosses right, talking to himself*) Professor Talmadge, head of the Department of Romance Languages, using such words!

MYRA   Leon, you're supposed to call all these numbers right away.
   (*She extends the list to him again*)

SOLOMON (*Ignoring the list*)   First things first. It seems to me that every time I come home lately, Albert is lying on the grass, being undignified and getting a temperature.

MYRA   Yes, and it's all your fault. I told the president of the Student Council—(*The telephone rings*) That must be for you, Leon.

SOLOMON   I'm not home yet.
   (*The telephone rings again*)

MYRA   But, Leon, they all say it's important.

SOLOMON   I'm not home yet.

TALL STORY

MYRA Shh! (*Into telephone*) Hello. Yes, I have your message. (MYRA *glances at* SOLOMON, *then turns her back on him*) I'll tell Professor Solomon the next time I see him. (*She hangs up*) That was Professor Alexander. He called three times.

SOLOMON Professor Alexander! He called three times, eh? I know—he wants to apologize!

MYRA Why should he apologize to you?

SOLOMON Why should he apologize to me? I'll tell you why. Because I told him to his face that he was an intellectual fraud.

MYRA Leon, is anything wrong?

SOLOMON Don't change the subject. Why is Albert's temperature my fault?

MYRA Because he has to play dead.

SOLOMON (*Crossing left*) Myra, I've had a trying day. Will you please make a little sense.

MYRA All right. All the children in the neighborhood have guns. Bang—bang—bang! You're against war. So the Solomon children can't have guns. What happens when they play? Bang—bang—bang! Albert gets killed right away. So there he is lying on the grass, dead, catching cold.
(ALBERT *comes down the stairs, with the thermometer in his mouth*)

SOLOMON How are you going to stop war if we encourage children to play with the instruments of war?

55

MYRA What's it got to do with war? All Albert wants to be is Wyatt Earp.
(SOLOMON *crosses right, looks from* MYRA *to* ALBERT, *then points to the stool down right center.* ALBERT *goes to the stool and sits*)

SOLOMON Albert, remember our talks about man being the first animal to have a freedom of choice—to know good from evil—and his slow rise in the spiritual scale, until today man's goal must be the preservation of peace? (ALBERT *tries to talk with the thermometer in his mouth*) Albert, don't mumble.
(ALBERT *takes the thermometer out*)

ALBERT Mitch Matthews has got a Wyatt Earp gun. It says right on the gun, "Peace Preserver."
(ALBERT *puts the thermometer back into his mouth*)

SOLOMON Albert, to put "Peace Preserver" on a gun is to betray the language. Don't be fooled by semantics. Do you know what semantic means?
(ALBERT *takes the thermometer out.* SOLOMON *takes it from him*)

ALBERT I know what anti-semantic means.
(SOLOMON *raises the thermometer in impatience.* MYRA *seizes it and takes it to the window, where she studies it*)

MYRA (*Reading thermometer*) Uh-huh. He *has* a temperature. Another cold.

SOLOMON (*Leaning down to* ALBERT's *level*) Albert, this is your opportunity to become a leader. You could persuade the boys they don't have to play games of violence. What's become of eenie-meenie-minie-moe?

TALL STORY

ALBERT   Father—that's for the immature.
   (MYRA *crosses to the table right of the sofa*)

MYRA   Leon, some other time. The boy's got a cold, and you've got all these calls to make.

SOLOMON (*Straightening up*)   Well, I'll say this—Albert doesn't catch colds at Fostoria.

MYRA (*To* ALBERT)   You go upstairs and—(*She starts* ALBERT *upstairs, then suddenly recalls* SOLOMON's *last remark. To* SOLOMON) Fostoria! Are you in trouble?

SOLOMON (*Postponing the issue*)   Albert, a man should always live up to the best that's in him.

MYRA   Leon, are you in trouble?

SOLOMON (*To* MYRA)   No man who lives up to his principles is in trouble.

MYRA   You're in trouble.
   (MYRA *crosses left, worried*)

SOLOMON (*To* ALBERT)   Always remember this: "To thine own self be true." That's Shakespeare.

ALBERT (*At foot of stairs*)   I thought you didn't like Shakespeare.

SOLOMON   I like Shakespeare. I just don't like the Drama Department.

ALBERT   What Drama Department?

SOLOMON (*Testily*)   Any drama department. Go upstairs and go to bed. You've got a temperature.

TALL STORY

ALBERT   How high is it?

MYRA   Never mind. It's almost a hundred.

ALBERT   The highest fever anyone in our class ever had was a hundred and five. I'd like to beat that.

MYRA   Don't say such a thing.

ALBERT   You always want me to get high marks.
   (ALBERT *disappears upstairs.* SOLOMON *picks up the list of telephone calls from the table*)

MYRA (*After a pause*)   Leon, did you flunk somebody?

SOLOMON   Myra, you know my principle. I will not discuss my scholastic affairs in the home.

MYRA   You haven't got a son or daughter of a trustee in your—

SOLOMON (*Discovering a name on the list*)   The president of the Student Council! In what kind of an age are we living? Where has it gone, Myra, the great respect that the teacher once commanded?

MYRA   You mean at Ohio State?

SOLOMON   I mean in Athens—in Rome! Where has it gone, the authority of the informed man? Who would have dared question Plato's estimate of his pupil Aristotle. Would Thomas Aquinas, under pressure, have changed a C plus to a B minus?

MYRA   Leon, you did flunk somebody! I don't mean anybody— I mean somebody!
   (SOLOMON *crushes the list and throws it down*)

TALL STORY

SOLOMON They don't know me, that's all—they just don't know me! (SOLOMON *strides to the door, throws it open and addresses the world*) I stand for academic integrity!

MYRA Leon, you didn't flunk the whole class?
  (SOLOMON *closes the door and recovers his poise*)

SOLOMON I'm going upstairs.

MYRA Leon, you told me at Grinnell, you told me at North Dakota, you told me at Oberlin—you can tell me here.

SOLOMON Please! I have a splitting headache. I'm going up and lie down.

MYRA All right. Maybe a nap will do you good. And I've got to get a baby sitter. We're going to Charlie Osman's to dinner.

SOLOMON Tonight I'm not going anywhere.
  (*He disappears upstairs*)

MYRA But after dinner we're all going to the basketball game.

SOLOMON (*Off; as though stung*) Oh, no!

MYRA But Leon—
  (SOLOMON *comes back into sight and speaks with an obvious effort at control*)

SOLOMON In this college there's too much emphasis on basketball!
  (*He continues on upstairs*)

MYRA Leon, tonight the emphasis *should* be on—(*The importance of basketball looms before her; as she turns front,*

TALL STORY

gradually the light dawns. She makes the gesture of height)
Ray Blent!
  (*She sinks to the couch, her hand on her head*)

Curtain

ACT TWO

Scene 1

The living room of PROFESSOR OSMAN's *home. The same afternoon. It is a well-appointed room. Wherever the wall is not recessed into a bookcase, it is paneled. There is a fireplace up center. The door to the foyer is left of this fireplace. The door to the kitchen is down right. It is perhaps the slightly Gothic touch of the architraves of the doors that suggests this apartment might possibly be in a dormitory. Right of center is a table-desk, with a telephone and the usual desk accessories. Left of the desk, at about stage center, is a Windsor armchair. Down stage against the left wall is a small cabinet of bric-a-brac, above this a comfortable upholstered armchair. Between this chair and the door to the foyer is a liquor cabinet. On the liquor cabinet are bottles of Scotch, bourbon and brandy, and some old-fashioned glasses. Inside the cabinet are some brandy glasses. There is a side chair below the door down right.*

At rise: CHARLES OSMAN *is seated at the table-desk. Clustered around the desk are the basketball players, in uniform, with their overcoats on. The telephone is ringing.*

MYERS We're not talking just for the team, Mr. Osman.

BAKER We're talking for the whole campus—the whole college.

SIMPSON How could you possibly see Ray Blent's name on a test and flunk him? (*The phone rings again*) And before the season's over!

TALL STORY

WRIGHT   Yeah—how could you?
(OSMAN *takes the receiver off the hook, and puts it on the desk*)

OSMAN   I always grade an examination paper before I look to see who has written it.

BAKER   Then you didn't know it was Ray Blent's paper!

GRANT   Oh, well! All you have to do is look at the paper again, now that you know it's Blent's and pass him.

WRIGHT   See how simple it is, Mr. Osman?

OSMAN   No. When a boy as bright as Blent turns in that bad a paper, he deserves the lowest mark I can give him.

WRIGHT   Wait a minute, Mr. Osman!

GRANT   Chalky, I've got to agree with Mr. Osman. He couldn't go over that exam and change the grade. It wouldn't look good. But I've got a better idea.

WRIGHT   What is it?

GRANT   (*To* OSMAN)   Give him another exam—a make-up exam. (*He looks at his watch*) And you haven't got much time.

BAKER   That does it!

SIMPSON   Yeah—that's perfect!

GRANT   Look—we'll send Blent right over.
(*The team starts for the door.* OSMAN *raises his hand and his voice*)

OSMAN   Whoa! (*They stop.* OSMAN *rises and goes toward them*) What if he doesn't pass that exam?

64

TALL STORY

GRANT I've got that figured out, too, Mr. Osman. You don't grade it until Monday.

OSMAN (*With a touch of irony*) Do you think it would be absolutely honest to play it that way, Grant?

GRANT Well, I'll say this—it would be the right thing to do, under the circumstances, and the generous thing.

OSMAN Oh, I see. I'm to be right and generous all weekend and then start being honest, say, about ten o'clock Monday morning. (OSMAN *goes to the liquor cabinet and takes a bottle and glass*) I know all you boys are in training.
(*He pours himself a drink and puts down the bottle*)

WYMAN I'm not in training.
(OSMAN *studies him a moment*)

OSMAN You're Wyman, aren't you?

WYMAN Yes, sir.

OSMAN I flunked you, too, didn't I?

WYMAN Yes, sir.

OSMAN (*To the others*) Why shouldn't I give him a make-up exam?

BAKER Because he's a lousy player!
(SIMPSON *notices* OSMAN's *phone is off the cradle*)

SIMPSON Sir! You know your phone is off the hook.

OSMAN (*Sharply*) Yes, and leave it off!
(OSMAN *starts back to the desk*)

MYERS   Let's be serious, Mr. Osman. You don't know how the students feel about Ray Blent. To us he represents just about the same things as the man the college was named for—General George Armstrong Custer.

OSMAN (*Below the desk*)   I see what you mean. General Custer was dashing, fearless, a popular hero—and died an early death because of lack of information.

GRANT   Don't kid about this, Mr. Osman. When you mention Custer anywhere in this country what's the first thing people think of? Basketball! And when they think of basketball they think of Ray Blent. He's responsible for Custer's reputation today.

OSMAN (*As if impressed*)   What you're saying is that a good basketball center is really an academic achievement.

GRANT   Yeah! Only you said it better than I could. I'm glad you understand!

BAKER   It's all settled then, is it, Mr. Osman?

OSMAN   Yes, it's all settled.
   (*The boys shout with joy and again start for the door, except* SIMPSON, *who remains above the desk*)

SIMPSON   What'll we tell Blent?

OSMAN   Tell him he's still ineligible. (*With this there is a terrific burst of protest from the squad, each member rising to a crescendo of considerable volume, as they rush back and surround* OSMAN. *At the height of this hubbub* COACH HARDY *enters and blows his whistle. They all stop talking and give*

TALL STORY

a startled look to HARDY) Thank God, the first half's over! (OSMAN *walks away from the boys to down left*)

HARDY   I could hear you boys clear out on the sidewalk. How dare you yell at Professor Osman! What are you doing here, anyway?

BAKER   Well, Coach, you told us—

HARDY   (*Cutting in quickly*)   I told you Blent was ineligible, but that didn't mean—Mr. Osman, have they tried to put pressure on you?

OSMAN   I think it could be described that way.

HARDY   I'm shocked! I apologize. (*To the boys*) Why aren't you at the gymnasium? I've been looking all over the campus for you. Get back there instanter—

WYMAN   How?

HARDY   Right away! And wait there for me. (*They begin to file out*) I'm ashamed of you—all of you. (*To* OSMAN) I'm sorry this happened. The minute I turn my back—(*The last of the squad has gone*) When you get a bunch of wild kids like that you can't always control them.

OSMAN   On the contrary it seemed to me they showed very good teamwork. And now what can I do for you and don't think I'm going to do it.

HARDY   Professor Osman, believe me, I didn't come here about Blent. (*Rather than argue,* OSMAN *walks past* HARDY *toward his desk*) I knew the team was upset and I was afraid they might be in your hair. (*Realizing too late that* OSMAN *is bald*) Oh, I beg your pardon . . . I didn't mean that . . .

OSMAN Tell me something—is Blent so important? Can any one man be so important?

HARDY I have to admit he's pretty important. In a small school like this, you know, you don't have much depth.

OSMAN Yes, I've found that to be true.

HARDY I didn't know you realized that. You see, you professors lead a kind of protected life. Sure, you don't get as much dough as I do, but you don't have to compete. I have to compete. Blent makes Custer look good, and when Custer looks good I look good.

OSMAN (*Looking toward the kitchen*) Will you excuse me a minute? I'm in danger of not looking good. I'm expecting some guests for dinner and I have something on the stove.
   (*He starts toward the kitchen, putting his glass of whiskey on the desk*)

HARDY I've got to run along, anyway. I'll let myself out.

OSMAN Fine!
   (*He exits to the kitchen*)

HARDY Sorry the boys ganged up on you. Personally, I wouldn't think of trying to influence you. Just let your conscience be your guide . . .

OSMAN (*Off*) Thank you. And I hope Custer wins.
   (*There is a knock on the door.* HARDY *opens the door and finds* PRESIDENT NAGEL)

HARDY (*Lowering his voice*) Good! You're here! Come in— he's in the kitchen. (*Calling out*) Mr. Osman, who do you think I found on your doorstep? President Nagel.

TALL STORY

NAGEL Hello, Charles.

OSMAN (*Off*) Hello, Harmon. Make yourself at home. I'll be with you in a few minutes.

HARDY The boys didn't get anywhere with him.

NAGEL They shouldn't have tried.

HARDY But you can bring him into line, can't you?

NAGEL Yes, I think I can. Of course he'll make me squirm first. Sandy, that's how a college president gets most of his exercise—squirming.

HARDY How about the other fellow?

NAGEL I can't deal with him directly. But I've got an idea.

HARDY Yeah?

NAGEL I'll have to work through someone else. Sandy, get out of here.

HARDY You know the game's tonight.

NAGEL I'll do what I can. But I'll have to play it by ear. Now run along, Sandy! (HARDY *lets himself out.* NAGEL *raises his voice*) Something smells good, Charles.

(NAGEL *removes his topcoat and drops it and his hat in the armchair left*)

OSMAN (*Appearing in an apron and carrying a spoon*) I'll be with you in a second.

NAGEL No hurry.

OSMAN I have some guests coming to dinner. (*He starts back*

to the kitchen) I've had a busy afternoon—and it's damn near ruined this beef Stroganoff.
(*He is off*)

NAGEL You may have your troubles, but at least you're not a college president. I've had a hell of a day.

OSMAN (*Off*) Sorry.
(NAGEL *stretches out in the chair left of the desk*)

NAGEL Oh, no, it wasn't just that. One of our charges is now under police charges. Young Manson. Last night he got drunk and parked his car in a space already occupied by a police car.

OSMAN (*Entering*) I can see why that was brought to your attention.
(*He removes his apron and drops it in the chair down right*)

NAGEL The student's parents have been on the phone all day to assure me their boy does not own an automobile, has never learned to drive, and has never taken a drink.

OSMAN Uh-huh. Tell me some more of your troubles.
(OSMAN *perches on a corner of the desk*)

NAGEL All right. Why should I, with everything happening at once, have to spend two hours getting Mrs. Parrish seats for the game tonight?

OSMAN Mrs. Parrish?

NAGEL She's the widow of a trustee. He died in nineteen thirty-seven.

TALL STORY

OSMAN Well, Harmon, I'm all for trustees having widows.

NAGEL So am I. But Mrs. Parrish has a great deal of money which at present she plans to leave to Custer.

OSMAN Very interesting. But, Harmon, do you need so large a bush to beat about?

NAGEL Charles, I mentioned the Parrish fortune because most colleges depend on legacies to keep going. And, Charles, we academicians are so afraid of the power of money limiting academic freedom that we overlook one thing. Without money there would be very little academic freedom because there would be practically nothing academic.

OSMAN And what has all this to do with the young man whose name we are so carefully avoiding?

NAGEL All right, let's mention it. Since Ray Blent has been playing basketball here, this little college of ours has become nationally prominent. Now we're suddenly getting some of the best student material from all over the country. Because of all this we've been able to raise our scholastic standards.

OSMAN (*Rising*) Yes, and I must give you credit, Harmon. You led the fight for higher standards.

NAGEL Thank you, Charles. It's good to hear you say that.

OSMAN And may I remind you, the rule that failure in only one subject would make an athlete ineligible was, as I remember, your idea?
(OSMAN *picks up his drink*)

NAGEL Yes, damn it.

TALL STORY

OSMAN Well, I guess that takes care of Blent. It was nice of you to drop in, Harmon.

(*He pats* NAGEL *on the shoulder and goes up to the liquor cabinet, where he puts down his glass*)

NAGEL (*Rising and going to* OSMAN) But, Charles, some things have happened which none of us could foresee. You may not welcome this information, but I have to report that since Blent has been playing basketball our contributions from the alumni have more than tripled.

OSMAN Harmon, I should think you would know me well enough to realize that I will have to resist to the death any administrative pressure.

NAGEL But, Charles, we've been talking as old friends.

OSMAN (*A twinkle in his eye*) Harmon, you misled me entirely. I thought you said something about being the president of this college.

NAGEL Only to tell you my troubles. I want to make this clear, Charles. You were perfectly within your competence in flunking the boy if he wrote a bad exam. But if you did decide to give Blent a make-up exam, there are plenty of precedents for that. However, I'm not here to put pressure on you.

OSMAN Harmon, you're the seventh man today who's assured me he wasn't trying to put pressure on me.

NAGEL Charles, I'm sorry! I should have realized what a tough day you've had. I shouldn't have come here. (*As if accepting the defeat*) You know, when I joined this—this mendicant order of college presidents, I thought the only thing I'd have

TALL STORY

to beg for would be money. Forget the whole thing. I'm sorry. (*He starts for his hat and coat*)

OSMAN   Now wait a minute, Harmon. You and I have never been too far apart in our devotion to Custer. (NAGEL *stops*) Let me be sure I'm clear about this—Were you trying to say that we two are so intelligent, so human, and so full of wisdom, that we can agree to give the boy a chance?

NAGEL   That was my underlying thought.

OSMAN   Well, I'm glad to agree with you that we're both intelligent men.

NAGEL   Uh-huh.

OSMAN   And I can practically go along with you on the theory that we're both human.

NAGEL   Charles, I think together we're beginning to make sense.

OSMAN   I know you wouldn't expect me to promise anything, because if you did, I'd have to say no. Let's just say I've agreed to think it over.

NAGEL   (*Relieved*)   Thank you, Charles. I knew you'd see the whole picture.

OSMAN   You know, Harmon, in some circles you'd be known as a smooth operator.

NAGEL   No—no! And it's a comfort to have on the faculty a man such as you—a reasonable man whose opinion the other professors respect. Which reminds me, I have a further problem that has to be solved—well, immediately. Perhaps you could help me. How should I go about—(*He stops, looks around and listens a moment*) Charles, have you by any chance discovered uranium?

OSMAN (*Surprised*) No, I haven't even tried.

NAGEL Ever since I've been here I've been hearing a Geiger counter.

OSMAN Oh, it's the telephone. I took the receiver off the hook—in the hope of getting myself off the hook.

NAGEL I told Miss Federman if she had to reach me I'd be here.

OSMAN I'm sorry. (OSMAN *puts the receiver back on its cradle. It rings immediately*) Someone else who doesn't want to put pressure on me.

NAGEL I'll tell them you're out. (*He answers the phone*) Hello. (*To* OSMAN) It's a woman. (*Into telephone*) I'm not sure. May I ask who's calling? (*Pause*) Just a moment. (*To* OSMAN) It's a Myra somebody.

OSMAN Oh! It's Myra Solomon . . . Professor Solomon's wife . . . I'll tell her I'll call her back later.

NAGEL Oh, no! Go ahead and talk to her. (*He hands the phone to* OSMAN) As a matter of fact—it just happened that I was—

OSMAN (*Into telephone*) Hello, Myra . . . (*Very distressed*) Oh, no, Myra—I've been working on this dinner for two days. (*Pause*) You must be able to find a baby sitter somewhere. Keep on trying! Myra, I'll even let you do the dishes. (*Pause*) I'm going to expect you at six. (*Pause*) Myra, please, it's beef Stroganoff, my masterpiece. Keep trying. (*He hangs up*) Damn!

TALL STORY

NAGEL (*Strolling center*) I understand you've made quite a friend of Professor Solomon.

OSMAN Yes, he's very well worth knowing.

NAGEL I haven't been able to get acquainted with him. Good teacher, you know. I've found that in most courses in ethics the students end up so bewildered they no longer know right from wrong.

OSMAN Not Leon's students. You might give him a thought for the chair in that department.

NAGEL Oh? Your opinion would carry considerable weight. Too bad he's going to miss one of your dinners. (*He takes a pause*) Oh, may I use your phone?

OSMAN Help yourself.
(NAGEL *goes to the phone and dials a number.* OSMAN *crosses and recovers his drink*)

NAGEL (*To* OSMAN) Well, if you have that great a respect for Solomon, I'm sure he must have a high regard for you. (*Into phone*) Miss Federman, Mrs. Nagel and I were to dine with the Wentworths tonight, weren't we? (*Pause*) Well, would you call Mrs. Nagel and tell her we'll have to cancel it. And didn't I hear you arrange for a baby sitter for us tonight? (*Pause*) No, don't cancel her—but get in touch with her and tell her to report to Professor Solomon's house instead. They'll be expecting her. I'll be right back at the office. (*He hangs up*) Well, Charles, your dinner won't go to waste after all. You just call Mrs. Solomon and tell her you've arranged for a baby sitter.

OSMAN Thanks, Harmon. You didn't have to go to all that trouble.

(NAGEL *picks up his hat and puts his coat on*)

NAGEL I'm glad it worked out this way. Oh! Some people are dropping over to my house after the game tonight—that is, if we win. Why don't you come along and bring the Solomons?

OSMAN I wouldn't count on the Solomons, Harmon.

NAGEL Do try. Well, at least they'll be here for dinner and that will give you a chance to put your point of view before Solomon.

OSMAN My point of view? About what?

NAGEL About Blent.

OSMAN Blent?

NAGEL Yes—as you were saying to me—the intelligent thing to do, the human thing—you know!

OSMAN Why should I say all that to Solomon?

NAGEL Well, you see, Charles, Solomon flunked Blent, too. I'm sure everything's safe in your hands. See you later.

(*He goes out.* OSMAN *walks to the telephone and dials a number. While he is waiting he turns and looks at the door and smiles faintly*)

OSMAN No wonder the son-of-a-bitch is president!

The Lights Black Out

Scene 2

The Solomon living room. Later that afternoon.
At rise: ALBERT, *dressed in his pajamas and dressing gown, is sitting on the couch, thermometer in mouth.* MYRA *is at the telephone.*

MYRA (*Into telephone*) I did expect him . . . The minute he steps foot in this room I'll tell him you called! Can I tell him what it's about? . . . All right. Thank you. Good-bye. (*She hangs up*) Why won't anybody tell me what it's about even though I think I know what it's about? (ALBERT *mumbles to her*) It's not going to get any higher just because you take it every five minutes.
(*She takes the thermometer out and looks at it*)

ALBERT Is it more or less?

MYRA More or less.

ALBERT I mean is it up or down?

MYRA It's the same.

ALBERT (*Disappointed*) Aw! I'm no good at anything.
(*He takes the thermometer and goes to the foot of the stairs*)

MYRA Get back to bed and keep away from the other children.

ALBERT Can't I kiss them good night?

MYRA   With a temperature, never kiss anybody. You might give them what you've you got. Go to bed.

ALBERT   Is it measles?

MYRA   You've had measles.

ALBERT   Could it be a rare tropical disease?

MYRA   How could you get a rare tropical disease?

ALBERT   Well, in "Ramar of the Jungle" somebody's always getting a rare tropical disease.

MYRA   With you children I know this house is a jungle, but it's not tropical. Go upstairs and get into bed.
   (SOLOMON *comes downstairs. He sees* ALBERT)

SOLOMON   Myra, why is Albert down here? Why isn't he in bed?

MYRA   Leon, some day I'll teach ethics and you take care of Albert. I told him twelve times.

SOLOMON   Albert, go to bed.

ALBERT   (*Promptly*)   Yes, sir.
   (ALBERT *goes upstairs*)

SOLOMON   He's an obedient child. He's no trouble.

MYRA   How's your headache? I mean the one in your head.

SOLOMON   I couldn't get any rest with the telephone ringing all the time.
   (*The telephone rings.* MYRA *answers it*)

TALL STORY

MYRA (*Into telephone*) Hello ... Who? ... Anderson? No, there's no one by that name here ... (*She hangs up and speaks to* SOLOMON) That was nice for a change. Wrong number ... (*She picks up a new list from the table, and extends it, tentatively*) Here's the names of while you were upstairs.

SOLOMON I don't want to see them.

MYRA One was Charlie Osman. He's got the dinner all cooked. He even found a baby sitter for us. It wouldn't put you under any obligation—he just likes you.
  (*The telephone rings*)

SOLOMON I'm going to bed. (*The telephone rings again*) I'm in bed.
  (MYRA *answers the telephone.* SOLOMON *lingers to listen*)

MYRA (*Into telephone*) Hello ... (*She listens, then nods several times*) I'll tell him. He'll call you back. (*She hangs up*) I guess that's going to keep up all night.

SOLOMON We'll go to Osman's.

MYRA (*Fishing*) Do we go to the basketball game afterwards?

SOLOMON Myra, conversation has become a lost art. We'll just sit and talk to Osman.
  (*The doorbell rings*)

MYRA Now it's the doorbell. They're closing in on us. You go on upstairs. I'll answer it.

SOLOMON No! I don't hide in my own house.
  (*He opens the door and* JUNE RYDER *is standing there*)

TALL STORY

JUNE Good evening, Professor Solomon. May I come in? (*She does*)

SOLOMON It won't do you any good. Young lady, I will not have anyone come into my own house and put pressure on me. That's final. You may as well go.

JUNE But, Mr. Solomon, I'm your baby sitter.

SOLOMON Come in, we've been waiting for you.

JUNE (*To* MYRA) Good evening, Mrs. Solomon.

MYRA Haven't I met you?

JUNE Yes, I'm June Ryder. I just got a telephone call to report to you right away.

MYRA It was in that restaurant—that College Café.

JUNE That's right.

MYRA And you were with—
(*She gestures height*)

JUNE Yes.

MYRA So that's what my husband thought you were here on account of. (*To* SOLOMON) You flunked Ray Blent!

SOLOMON He failed to pass his examination.

MYRA On the day of the big game you flunked—(*She makes the gesture of height*) Ray Blent!

JUNE Mrs. Solomon, I'm sure your husband was fair. Ray Blent hasn't been—Ray Blent lately.
(SOLOMON *feels he has scored a small triumph*)

TALL STORY

SOLOMON If we're dining at Professor Osman's I'd better wash up.

(He exits upstairs)

MYRA *(To herself)* Oh, well, it will be good to see our old friends at Fostoria again. (ALBERT *comes through the kitchen door with the thermometer in his mouth*) Albert, you're supposed to be in bed. Go back there! Come here! This is the baby sitter.

JUNE Hello, little man. How are you?
(ALBERT takes the thermometer out of his mouth and hands it to JUNE)

ALBERT I've got a fever. See?

JUNE *(Reading thermometer)* That's not very much.

ALBERT *(Belligerently)* Well, it's above ninety-nine, isn't it?

JUNE A little.

ALBERT Well, then I've got a fever. What's your name?

MYRA Albert, this is Miss Ryder. And you go back to bed and don't come down again tonight.
(MYRA leads ALBERT toward the stairs)

ALBERT I want a drink of water.
(He starts for the kitchen)

MYRA *(Pulling him back)* There's water in the bathroom.

ALBERT Daddy's in the bathroom.

MYRA He'll be out before you die of thirst. Get back upstairs.
(ALBERT goes up reluctantly. MYRA takes JUNE'S coat

TALL STORY

and hangs it on the hat rack. JUNE *searches for something nice she can say about* ALBERT)

JUNE He's a—quite a boy for his age. How old is he?

MYRA Ten. Take his temperature again before you go and if it's really high call me at Professor Osman's—the number is four-seven-two-o. (JUNE *takes a pad and pencil out of her handbag and makes a note*) But if anyone telephones don't give that number. We're out for the evening, but you don't know where.

JUNE Yes, Mrs. Solomon.

(MYRA *leads* JUNE *to the couch, where they sit*)

MYRA I'll tell you about the children. Ruth's doing her homework and she'll go to bed herself. So will Joel. Debbie's in the bathtub. Ruth will dry her off and put her to bed. The twins, William and Mary, they're asleep now and never any bother.

JUNE You know I'll have to leave at eight o'clock.

MYRA My cleaning woman—Mrs. Lindstrom—will be here at eight o'clock, maybe before.

JUNE I'm one of the cheer leaders.

MYRA I don't think there'll be much cheering tonight. Ray Blent he flunked. You know who Leon flunked at Cranford? The daughter of the chairman of the board of trustees. So she eloped with a truck driver. They found the truck later halfway across the country. (SOLOMON *enters down the stairs*) Leon, where did they find that truck?

(SOLOMON *looks pained that* MYRA *should have revived this incident*)

TALL STORY

SOLOMON   If we're going to Charlie Osman's you'd better get ready.

MYRA   (*To* JUNE)   You come up and meet the other children, and I'll show you where the bathroom is.
(*They start up*)

SOLOMON   Myra, people know a bathroom when they see it. Can't we get started?

MYRA   Leon, I'll only be a minute. If the phone rings, let it ring. (*She and* JUNE *exit upstairs.* SOLOMON *puts on his topcoat. The telephone rings. He starts for the stairs. At the foot of the stairs he pauses, regains his courage, walks with determination to the phone. Meantime, it has rung several times*)

SOLOMON   (*Into phone, brusquely*)   Professor Solomon speaking! . . . Hello . . . Hello . . . Hello . . . (*Obviously the phone is dead. He looks at the receiver contemptuously*) Coward! (*He hangs up. The doorbell rings. With his new courage he strides across the room and throws open the door.* RAY BLENT *is standing there*) Oh, it's you, young man. Step in.

RAY   (*Stepping in*)   Professor Solomon—

SOLOMON   I'm glad you're here. It is to your credit that you had the courage to face me.

RAY   Professor Solomon—

SOLOMON   Young man, if you have learned anything from my course you should have learned that man is a moral creature, and as a moral creature, must take the consequences of his actions.

TALL STORY

RAY   Yes, sir, but that's—

SOLOMON   You will wait until I finish. You turned in an inexcusably careless paper. You are a man of good equipment. It is unethical for a man so well endowed to turn in so irresponsible a paper. It would have been unethical of me to grade it in any other way than I did—

RAY   But, Professor Solomon—

SOLOMON   —just as it would be immoral of me to give any consideration whatever to the effect of my action on your athletic standing or eligibility. Blent, I hope what I have said has made some impression on you.

RAY   Sir, I wasn't exactly listening. I came here to talk to your baby sitter.
   (*This stops* SOLOMON *short in his tracks. He searches his mind for an appropriate comment*)

SOLOMON   Domestic matters are in the hands of my wife. Myra!

MYRA   (*Off*)   I'm ready—I'm ready!
   (*She enters down the stairs*)

RAY   Mrs. Solomon, I'm Ray Blent. Remember? Would you do me a favor?
   (MYRA *hurries to* SOLOMON's *side*)

MYRA   Right or wrong, I stand by my husband.

RAY   It's not about that. I know you're going out. But do you mind if I stay here and talk to Miss Ryder . . . your baby sitter?

MYRA Leon, isn't that sweet? In his trouble, he comes to talk to his girl. Doesn't that melt your heart?
  (*She looks at him hopefully*)

SOLOMON (*After a pause*) No!
  (SOLOMON *goes out the front door.* MYRA *looks at* RAY *and shrugs. She calls up the stairs*)

MYRA Miss Ryder, there's a young man here to see you. (*To* RAY) Good-bye!
  (MYRA *exits.* RAY *takes from his pocket a piece of paper to which is pinned a fraternity pin. He walks across the room looking at it.* JUNE *appears on the stairs. They see each other*)

JUNE (*Tearfully*) Ray, you shouldn't have come here. I wish you'd go. It's all over.

RAY I'll go. I just have to be clear about something. Come down a minute, will you please?
  (JUNE *comes down the stairs*)

RAY When I got back to the fraternity house I found my pin.

JUNE I left it there.

RAY Does your sending back my pin mean what I think it means—that we're not engaged any more?

JUNE Yes, it does! I'm not good for you, Ray.

RAY June, you can't do this!

JUNE Ray, let's not have a scene.

TALL STORY

RAY   There's not going to be any scene. I'm going to prove to you that this can't be—and I'm going to prove it logically.

JUNE   Ray—

RAY   Just a minute. This doesn't concern just you and me. This may turn out to have cosmic importance. You'd better sit down. (JUNE *sits*. RAY *speaks with great confidence*) Let me tell you something. When I discovered that we were both in love with each other, it presented a very interesting problem in physics.

JUNE   Physics?

RAY   Yes. I knew that governing all this there were natural laws.

JUNE   Ray, when two people fall in love—

RAY   Let me finish. (*As he speaks* RAY *takes off his topcoat, crosses left and drops it on the chair down left*) I sat down and started a fully documented treatise on the way we felt and why we felt that way.

JUNE (*Dismayed*)   You're not going to read it to me!

RAY   No. It isn't quite finished yet. When I got to the analysis of the phenomenon of why we're attracted to each other I found myself right on the edge of a terrific discovery! (*With momentary excitement*) You see, there's still one big thing that scientists aren't sure of yet—what holds the atom together—what is the basic magnetic attraction? Well, it could be the same natural law, the same power that holds men and women together. I haven't put my finger on it yet—but this could be revolutionary. And, June, that's why we have to go on! If you

break our engagement—June, you can't do this to science! You can't! You can't! (*He breaks emotionally*) June—I love you. That's all I've been trying to say.
    (*He sinks onto the couch and buries his head in his hands.* JUNE *moves over and puts her arms around him*)

JUNE Oh, Ray. You can't explain us that way. You know you're a little crazy—but the crazier you are the more I love you. (RAY *slowly comes out of his despair and looks at her*) There's nothing science can do about that.
    (*They go into an embrace and he covers her face with kisses.* ALBERT *enters from the kitchen. He goes over and touches* RAY *on the shoulder*)

ALBERT Have you got a temperature?
    (*Startled,* RAY *detaches himself from* JUNE *and turns*)

RAY What?

ALBERT If you've got a temperature you're not supposed to kiss anybody. They might catch it!

JUNE (*Leading* ALBERT *to the stairs*) You get upstairs into your bed or you're going to catch it.

ALBERT (*At top of the stairs*) Apparently you have no respect for human dignity.

JUNE You go to bed!
    (ALBERT *exits*)

RAY A kid like that makes you stop and think, doesn't it?

JUNE Let's not stop and think.
    (*She runs back into* RAY'S *embrace*)

TALL STORY

RAY Oh, June, I'm so sorry for what I put you through.

JUNE It's all right now. Everything's all right now.

RAY (*Formally*) Miss Ryder, would you wear my fraternity pin?

JUNE (*Tremulously*) Mr. Blent, I'd be pleased to.
(*He pins it on her*)

RAY When I got back to my room and found my pin, I was ready to die. I thought I'd lost you.

JUNE Darling, nothing like this must ever happen to us again.

RAY We've got to be sure it won't.

JUNE We've just got to. Let's get married right away.

RAY Right away?

JUNE Yes. Tonight!

RAY Tonight? But, Juney, we haven't any home. That's what you wanted.

JUNE I want you more than anything.

RAY All right. But, June . . .

JUNE What?
(RAY *turns away from her*)

RAY Well, first I've got to tell you something. I loved you so much—I wanted to get married so much—well, that fifteen hundred dollars didn't come from my uncle.

JUNE Where did it come from?

RAY I don't know.

JUNE You don't know!

RAY That's just it. I've got to—
(*There is a noise in the kitchen, which they both hear*)

JUNE Albert! I'll see to him. (*She marches toward the kitchen angrily and pushes open the door*) Albert Solomon! (*She stops short*) Oh, are you Mrs. Lindstrom?

WOMAN'S VOICE (*Off*) Yah!

JUNE Just a minute. I'll get my notebook. (*To* RAY *as she gets her notebook from the sofa*) Good, she's early. We can start right away. (*She starts for the kitchen. The telephone rings*) Take the telephone will you, Ray? Tell them the Solomons won't be back until late.
    (JUNE *exits into the kitchen.* RAY *goes to the phone and answers it*)

RAY (*Into telephone*) Hello. Professor Solomon's residence . . . Who? . . . I'm Ray Blent . . . Who's this? . . . Oh, you! How did you know I was here? . . . Look, I want to see you. I want to meet you some place . . . I thought you'd get in touch with me. When I flunked those exams I knew you'd want your money back . . . Wait a minute . . . I didn't do that to earn the money . . . I did that not to earn it . . . I don't know what you mean . . . Under the door?—what door? (*He looks toward the outside door. A Manila envelope has been pushed under it*) You wait a minute—you hold on! (*He goes to the front door, leans down, picks up the*

TALL STORY

envelope, opens it, and we see it is full of money. He rushes back to the telephone) Hey, where are you? You've got to take this back—you've got to take it all back—Hello—Hello—
(*He hangs up, and for a moment is bewildered*)

JUNE (*Off*) Good night, Mrs. Lindstrom. (JUNE *rushes for her coat and* RAY *for his, coming around the right end of the couch. To avoid a collision he has to leap over the stool*) It's all set—we can start. Gee, I've got goose pimples!
(RAY *stuffs the envelope into his overcoat pocket*)

RAY I'll see you later.
(*He starts getting into his coat, and in his hurry has a little difficulty.* ALBERT *appears on the stairs, unnoticed by* RAY *or* JUNE)

JUNE You'll see me later?

RAY Where's Mr. Solomon?

JUNE At Professor Osman's.

RAY Good! I've got to see them both right away.

JUNE Ray! We're going to get married!
(*By this time* RAY *is in his coat and has started for the door*)

RAY What?
(JUNE *stops him*)

JUNE We're going to be married!

RAY (*Remembering*) Not tonight. Some other time. I've got to play in that game tonight. They've got to let me!

90

TALL STORY

JUNE   Ray! You're ineligible!

RAY   That's why I have to see them. There's something they don't know. I flunked those exams on purpose!
(*He dashes out the door, leaving it open*)

JUNE (*Going to the door*)   Ray! (ALBERT *comes down the stairs and kneels behind the open door to keep from being seen.* JUNE *turns back into the room in bewildered panic.* ALBERT *crawls out the open door.* JUNE, *having regained her indignation, starts out. Just as she gets through the open door, she stops short*) Albert! (*She runs back into the room, calling toward the kitchen*) Mrs. Lindstrom! Mrs. Lindstrom! Albert fell out the window!
(*She rushes out the door*)

The Lights Black Out

Scene 3

The living room of CHARLES OSMAN'S *home. Early that evening. Center is a card table spread with a tablecloth. At its left is the Windsor armchair; at its right is the side chair which had been below the door down right, and above the table is a similar armchair.*

At rise: MYRA *and* SOLOMON *are discovered sitting comfortably, looking replete and happy.* MYRA *is seated above the table and is sipping her coffee.* SOLOMON *is seated left of the table, smoking a cigar, relishing it as if it were an unaccustomed treat.*

MYRA   Leon, you should have majored in physics. What a dinner! And I'll bet he did the whole thing on a Bunsen burner. (*After a pause she looks toward the kitchen door, raising her voice*) Don't you touch those dishes, Charlie.

OSMAN (*Off*)   I won't. How's your coffee, Myra?

MYRA   Perfect. I like it strong.

OSMAN (*Off*)   Leon, I'll be right in with your Sanka.

SOLOMON   Sorry to be a trouble, Charles. I make it a rule never to drink coffee after dinner. It's a stimulant.

OSMAN (*Off*)   No trouble.

SOLOMON   What a fine man—so civilized. This afternoon at the Faculty Club half of the members cut me dead, and the other half jumped down my throat. We've had a nice quiet dinner. Has he once mentioned Blent? Not once.

Marc Connelly, Hans Conried and Marian Winters
as CHARLES OSMAN, LEON SOLOMON and MYRA SOLOMON

MYRA   How's your headache?

SOLOMON   What headache?
(OSMAN *enters with a large cup of Sanka. He puts it on the table in front of* SOLOMON *and crosses to the liquor cabinet*)

OSMAN   Here you are, Leon.

SOLOMON   Thank you.

OSMAN   A little brandy, Myra?

MYRA   No, thank you.

OSMAN   Leon?

SOLOMON   Yes, I think I'd like a little.
(OSMAN *pours two brandies*)

MYRA   (*To* SOLOMON)   Brandy's a stimulant.

SOLOMON   Myra, it has no caffein in it. (*To* OSMAN) This is very pleasant. What's the news on the science-research laboratory?
(OSMAN *puts a brandy down by* SOLOMON *and crosses behind the table and sits at its right*)

OSMAN   Making progress. They've raised enough money to go ahead with the building. To equip it we'll have to raise another quarter of a million. But Nagel's very good at that.

SOLOMON   Today science is fashionable. You can get anything for it.

MYRA   Pretty soon everybody will be a scientist. Who's going to collect the garbage?

TALL STORY

SOLOMON Still, a little overemphasis on science is a relief from overemphasis on athletics.

MYRA Leon, let's not mention athletics. You've had enough of that for one day.

OSMAN I thought of you a great many times today, Leon, and with considerable sympathy.

SOLOMON You're the only one. You don't know what a day I've had.

OSMAN I think I do.

SOLOMON You couldn't! I've never been so important since my bar mitzvah. Up to now nobody's cared about my mind. Now all of a sudden everybody wants me to change it. Charlie, have you any idea how important basketball is to academic life—to the development of the whole person? You should have heard! Do you know that what began at Pearl Harbor was finished in Madison Square Garden—that Plato said music *and* gymnastic—that Immanuel Kant invented the one hand overhead back shot?

OSMAN Now just a minute, Leon. As intelligent men we know there are two sides to everything.

SOLOMON Not in ethics—not the way I teach it.

OSMAN Don't tell me you believe in absolutes!

SOLOMON Absolutely!

MYRA (*Speaking from experience*) Absolutely!

TALL STORY

OSMAN Leon, I'd like to discuss this situation, if you don't mind.

SOLOMON I do—but go ahead.

OSMAN There are some people who believe sincerely that basketball has put Custer on the map.

SOLOMON Yes, some. But I'm glad to say not persons such as you and I.

OSMAN It isn't that simple. Since Custer's become important in the basketball picture, the alumni contributions have just about tripled.

SOLOMON Well, Charles, we both know what we think of the alumni.

MYRA It wasn't just the alumni Charlie mentioned. It was contributions.

SOLOMON So what?

MYRA So Charlie's new laboratory—maybe he wouldn't get it.

SOLOMON (*Indignant*) Now I *am* mad! Isn't that just like the alumni, Charles—to punish you for something I did.
  (SOLOMON *has risen and crossed to behind* OSMAN)

OSMAN It's not just what you did.

SOLOMON Of course it is. I'm the one that flunked Ray Blent.

OSMAN Leon, I flunked Ray Blent, too.

SOLOMON You flunked Ray Blent?

TALL STORY

MYRA You flunked Ray Blent, too?

OSMAN Yes.

SOLOMON Charles, I'm proud of you! (*He seizes* OSMAN's *hand and shakes it so vigorously that he shakes* OSMAN, *too*) Myra, here's a great man. He's risked his whole new laboratory to stand on his principles.

OSMAN (*Angrily*) It never occurred to me until this very moment to connect my flunking of Blent with the science-research program. Now you've made it damn difficult for me to say what I wanted to say.
(*He rises and crosses left*)

SOLOMON Why shouldn't you say it? I'm a reasonable man.

OSMAN I wanted to tell you that before I knew you were involved in this I'd just about made up my mind—to make it possible for Blent to play tonight.
(SOLOMON *crosses to* OSMAN's *right*)

SOLOMON (*Shocked*) Charles, this is a question of right and wrong.

OSMAN Is it really? I'm not so sure it's not relatively unimportant.

SOLOMON That's why it's important! It's only when the issue is unimportant that the principle stands out. "Right must prevail even though the heavens fall!"

MYRA And after the heavens fall, who's going to know who was right?

OSMAN Can't you have an open mind about this?

SOLOMON On a moral issue there's no such thing as an open mind.
  (SOLOMON *sits in his chair decisively*)

OSMAN Leon, on any issue—

SOLOMON Charles, this is a question of academic integrity! Academic integrity! That I'll fight for even if I stand alone.
  (*There is a pause while* OSMAN *crosses in worried thought to above the desk*)

OSMAN I can't let you stand alone.

MYRA Charlie, don't worry. If there's one thing Leon's used to it's standing alone. Leon would have been a great Christian martyr if he'd been a Christian.

OSMAN No, Myra. The way Leon feels, it was a lost cause even before I started. Ethically, he's right and I'm wrong. His position is the only honest one. (*To* SOLOMON) We'll stand together.

MYRA (*Rising*) Charlie, Leon spoke the truth. You're a great man. (*She kisses him, then starts toward the kitchen*) Where do you keep the dishpan?

OSMAN Under the sink.

MYRA That's where both of you are, too.
  (*She exits to the kitchen.* OSMAN *takes the brandy glasses over to the liquor cabinet*)

SOLOMON (*Riding high on the crest of the wave*) Charles, let's show them! Let's face them! Let's go down to that basketball game and watch Custer lose.
  (OSMAN *winces*)

TALL STORY

OSMAN Leon—is this trip necessary?

SOLOMON (*Rising and going to above the desk*) It's the categorical imperative! All of my academic life I've waited—
(*There is a knock on the door, then suddenly the door bursts open and an hysterical* RAY BLENT *is jet-propelled into the room*)

RAY Mr. Osman! Mr. Solomon! You've got to let me play tonight! You've got to!

OSMAN See here—

RAY (*Going to* SOLOMON) They think I'm a crook. I'm not a crook! I have to prove I'm not a crook! I've got to play!

SOLOMON Young man, young man—

OSMAN Take it easy, boy.
(*He goes over to behind the table*)

RAY You have to listen to me! You're the only two that can do this. And you've got to—you've got to declare me eligible!

OSMAN Blent, get ahold of yourself . . . Sit down.

RAY No, I won't—

OSMAN (*Forcefully*) Sit down!

RAY Yes, sir.
(*He sits right of the table*)

OSMAN Blent, Professor Solomon and I have just reviewed your case, and taking all the facts into consideration, we have concluded that there is no reason to change our decision.

RAY But you don't *know* all the facts!

SOLOMON There's only one fact we have to know—you failed your examinations.

RAY (*Going to* SOLOMON) That's just it—what you don't know is that I failed them on purpose.
  (*This doesn't register*)

SOLOMON The rules on eligibility are very clear. Whenever— (*He stops. Something has dimly reached his consciousness. He looks at* RAY, *then at* OSMAN)

OSMAN What was it you just said?

RAY I said I failed those exams—both of them deliberately—on purpose.

SOLOMON (*To* RAY) You flunked our exams intentionally?

RAY Yes, sir.

SOLOMON (*To* OSMAN) Charles, that's vandalism!

OSMAN (*Curtly, walking away to the left*) Blent, you've committed the most irresponsible act I've ever heard of in all my years as a teacher. The whole college has been on our necks —just because of some childish caprice on your part.

RAY But I wanted to become ineligible . . . I didn't want to play—

OSMAN In the name of heaven, why?
  (RAY *rises, takes out the first envelope he received, removes the $1,500 and spreads it on the table*)

RAY That's why! (SOLOMON *and* OSMAN *stare at the money and then at each other*) They gave me that to throw the game. Fifteen hundred dollars.

SOLOMON They—who's they?

RAY That's the trouble. I don't know.

OSMAN Somebody gives you that much money and you don't know who it was?

RAY It was on the telephone.

SOLOMON Blent, make sense! Nobody can give you fifteen hundred-dollar bills on the telephone!

RAY He told me about it on the telephone. It was in a restaurant—Mike's.

OSMAN Mike's?

RAY I was called to the telephone. Some guy I didn't know asked me to throw the game. He promised me fifteen hundred right away and twenty-five hundred later. I told him to go to hell. Then when I got my coat from the checkroom I felt something in my pocket and when I took it out it was that fifteen hundred dollars.

OSMAN But, Blent—why did you keep it?

RAY I didn't know who to give it back to. And—well, I'm going to be honest with you—(BLENT *goes down left*) I needed a lot of money for something I wanted very much. So I held onto it for two or three days. And then I knew I couldn't throw the game. But how was I going to get out of it? And then it came to me—if I flunked an exam I'd be ineligible—I

TALL STORY

couldn't play. Then they couldn't expect me to throw the game.

SOLOMON   Blent, after my lectures on ethical theory . . .

RAY   Mr. Osman, I wrote fourteen wrong answers on your exam. Then I remembered, you've always been nice to me. You might pass me to give me a break. So to be safe I flunked Mr. Solomon's examination, too. I knew he wouldn't even give Abraham Lincoln a break.

OSMAN   Blent, you're wrong about Professor Solomon. I'm sure he'd have had consideration for Abraham Lincoln.

SOLOMON   Not if he turned in a bad paper.

RAY   How about it, Mr. Osman? How about it?

OSMAN (*Above the table*)   But, Blent, if your way out of this was not to play, it seems to me you've solved your problem.

RAY   No, it's worse now. Look at this! (*He takes out the other envelope and spreads the $2,500 on the table*) This is the rest of the money—the twenty-five hundred dollars. They just sent it to me. Don't you see—they think I flunked just so Custer would lose—so they would win their bets. That's why I've got to play!
   (RAY *crosses right*)

SOLOMON (*Looking at the money*)   Four thousand dollars—a year's salary!

OSMAN (*Going to* RAY)   Young man, has it ever occurred to you that whoever paid you to make sure that Custer lost might be slightly annoyed if Custer happened to win? And

TALL STORY

if you helped them to win they might damn well take it out of your hide? Hadn't that ever occurred to you?

RAY (*Stopped cold for a moment*)   No. I never thought about that. But I can see that they might.

OSMAN   I can see that they *would*.

RAY (*After a moment*)   All right. That's a chance I've got to take! I'm willing to take a beating.

OSMAN   Good boy! (*He pats* RAY's *arms approvingly, then turns and slowly approaches* SOLOMON, *who is now above the table*) Well, Leon, I guess it's up to us.

SOLOMON (*Crossing to behind the desk*)   All this doesn't change the facts. Blent, you know the rules. There's a basic morality involved here.

OSMAN   Leon, for God's sake, we can't let him—

SOLOMON (*With a gesture of finality*)   No, Charles.

RAY (*Pleading*)   Professor Solomon!

SOLOMON (*Firmly*)   Sorry!

RAY (*After a moment of decision*)   All right! Then I know what I have to do. I'm going down to the gymnasium. I'm going out on that floor before the game starts and tell everybody what I've done—the whole thing—that's the only way I can clear myself with myself. The hell with both of you.
   (*He bolts through the door and out.* OSMAN *hurries over to the door too late to stop* RAY. *He turns and looks at* SOLOMON)

TALL STORY

OSMAN Leon, we can't let him do that.

SOLOMON Morally, we can't do anything else.

OSMAN (*Going to* SOLOMON) Morally, we've got to do something else. Do you know what that would do to this boy? No matter how much he explained, all that anybody would remember would be that once he sold out to crooks. The boy's made a mistake and the world could have fallen on his head. But it hasn't. Do you insist that it must?
    (*In trying to avoid* OSMAN's *arguments,* SOLOMON *has been walking away from him until he is on stage left*)

SOLOMON Charles, all my life I've lived by certain principles. I've got to live by them now.

OSMAN Leon, you're a snob!

SOLOMON (*Not believing this came from* OSMAN) I'm a what?

OSMAN You're an ethical snob!

SOLOMON (*Protesting*) You don't mean—

OSMAN You're a God-damn ethical snob! (SOLOMON, *stunned, sits in armchair left*) You're going to let a boy ruin his life to prove that you're philosophically right. The categorical imperative! That's all you can think about. Can't you just once consider the human equation?

SOLOMON Human equation?

OSMAN Whether we win or lose a basketball game doesn't make a damn bit of difference. But what happens to that boy does—and as a matter of fact, what happens to you.

TALL STORY

SOLOMON (*Surprised*)   What happens to me?

OSMAN   Yes, you.

SOLOMON   Charles, all that I've ever lived by—

OSMAN   I know—rules! Rules!

SOLOMON   Yes. And don't tell me rules were made to be broken.

OSMAN   Leon, we don't have to break any rules. There's no rule against make-up exams.

SOLOMON   Make-up exams?

OSMAN   They've been given before—plenty of them. Leon, Blent failed deliberately. We both know he could have passed. We could go down to the gymnasium. We could throw a couple of questions at him—a couple of easy questions—

SOLOMON (*Rising*)   Not me!

OSMAN   For God's sake, Leon—
   (SOLOMON *goes out into the foyer, gets his topcoat and comes back, putting it on*)

SOLOMON   Not me! I'll give him the ten stiffest question I can think of—if I can just think of them.

OSMAN   Let's go.
   (OSMAN *starts for his coat.* SOLOMON *is at the table, where his eyes fall on the money*)

SOLOMON   One minute, Charles, there's another principle involved here.

TALL STORY

OSMAN Oh, Leon, No!

SOLOMON This money—the people who paid it made a deal in good faith. They should know the deal's off, and they should have their money back.

OSMAN We don't know who they are!

SOLOMON Blent said he got the money at Mike's.

OSMAN Yes, Mike! He'd know where it came from. After the game—
(*He gets his coat and hat from the foyer*)

SOLOMON If I'm to be a party to this, before we give Blent his examination this money must go back.

OSMAN (*Putting on his coat*) All right! All right! (*He helps* SOLOMON *pick up the money*) We'll stop at Mike's on the way down.
(MYRA *enters, carrying a tray*)

MYRA (*She sees them with their coats on*) Is it time to go to the basketball game?

SOLOMON (*Right of table*) Not for you.

OSMAN (*Left of table*) We're slipping down to the gymnasium ahead of time to give a make-up exam. We're going to fix things so Ray Blent can play tonight.
(MYRA *crosses behind the desk and now sees a fistful of money in* OSMAN'S *hand*)

MYRA (*Behind the table*) Charlie! (OSMAN *hands his money to* SOLOMON, *who puts it with the money he has picked up and stuffs it in one of the envelopes*) Leon! Not you!
(SOLOMON *realizes what has crossed* MYRA'S *mind*)

SOLOMON Myra, no! Blent, the poor boy, took a bribe to throw the game.

OSMAN He couldn't go through with it. He flunked his exams on purpose. We're going to give him another chance.
(*He goes to the door*)

MYRA (*Surprised*) Leon—you're going to give him another chance?

SOLOMON Myra, we have to consider the human equation!

MYRA The human equation! Charlie, what have you done to him? For twelve years we've been married and I've had to live according to the rules of Plato, Aristotle, St. Augustine and Tom Dewey. And now you're going to be human. Well, you can't begin soon enough for me. Go ahead. Get started. I'm glad you finally found out about the human equation. I've known about it for a long time.
(*She waves him across to her left*)

SOLOMON Myra, you mustn't be a snob!
(OSMAN *and* SOLOMON *exit.* MYRA *starts to clear the table, putting the coffee cups on the tray. The telephone rings. She goes to answer it, still holding the tray*)

MYRA (*Into telephone*) Hello—(*Pause*) No, Professor Osman isn't here. (*Pause*) Oh, President Nagel! This is Myra Solomon . . . Professor Solomon's wife. (*Pause*) Well, he and Leon just left for the gymnasium. They're going to give Mr. Blent a make-up examination. (*Pause*) They ought to be there any minute . . . (*Pause*) I'm glad you're glad. (*Pause*) After the game? Oh, how nice of you! We'll be glad to come . . . Thank you. Good-bye.

TALL STORY

(She hangs up, suddenly notices something on the floor right of the table, picks up a hundred dollar bill, admires it for a moment, looks toward the door, then back at the bill, and after a moment thrusts it down into her cleavage, shrugs happily and starts for the kitchen)

Curtain

ACT THREE

Scene I

PRESIDENT NAGEL's *office. The same evening. The only furniture is* PRESIDENT NAGEL's *desk, with a desk chair and a chair for visitors at its left. On the desk is a telephone and an intercom or squawk box. On the wall behind the desk are drawn curtains covering a window; to the left of this is a single picture, probably of the founder of Custer College. Left of this, in the back wall—the only necessary wall—is a door.*

At rise: PRESIDENT NAGEL *is seated at his desk, where there is evidence that he has dined on a bottle of milk and a sandwich. He is on the telephone, waiting.*

NAGEL (*After a pause*)   Sandy? . . . Sandy, I've got some great news for you . . . Blent's going to play . . . I just heard this minute, Sandy. I've been sitting here sweating it out. (*There is a buzz on the squawk box . . .*) Hold on a minute, Sandy. (*He flips the switch on the squawk box and speaks into it*) Yes?.

SECRETARY'S VOICE (*On squawk box*)   Mr. Nagel, Prosecutor Davis is here. Could you see him right away?

NAGEL (*Into box*)   Certainly. Send him in. (*He switches off the box and goes back to the telephone*) Sorry, Sandy . . . What? . . . Charlie Osman and Solomon are on the way to the gymnasium now. They're going to give Blent a make-up exam. (WES DAVIS *steps in*) Hello, Wes. Be with you in a minute. (*Into telephone*) I'll be there as soon as I can get away. Maybe I can be of some help myself. (*He hangs up and turns to* WES DAVIS, *happily*) Glad to see you, Wes. I've got to run in a minute. Anything important?

DAVIS (*Gravely*)   I'm afraid it is, Mr. Nagel. I've got some bad news for you.

NAGEL   Wes, can it wait till tomorrow? You know there's the game tonight.

DAVIS   It's about the game. There's been a fix.

NAGEL   A what, Wes?

DAVIS   A fix. (NAGEL *looks blank*) There's been some money passed— some bribery—the game's been fixed.

NAGEL (*Shocked*)   I can't believe such a thing! Ashmore's always had a good clean record.

DAVIS   It isn't Ashmore that's been fixed—it's Custer.

NAGEL (*Rising*)   Wes, repeating that kind of rumor could do the college damage.

DAVIS   It isn't a rumor, Mr. Nagel. That's why I've come to you.

NAGEL   Just what have you got to go on?

DAVIS   I've got two men outside—detectives from the Chicago gambling squad. They're down here investigating this. I told them I wanted them to see you.

NAGEL   You mean right away? Why?

TALL STORY

DAVIS We've got to protect Custer if we can. I want to keep on the good side of these fellows. They're pretty impressed at the idea of meeting a college president.

NAGEL (*Impressed himself*) How refreshing! Let's have them in. (NAGEL *flips the squawk box and talks into it*) The two gentlemen who came with Mr. Davis—will you send them in please?

(DAVIS *walks away to the left of the door*)

SECRETARY'S VOICE (*On squawk box*) Yes, Mr. Nagel.

NAGEL (*Switches off the box. Sitting*) Who on earth would do such a thing?

DAVIS Professional gamblers, Mr. Nagel.

NAGEL Gamblers! One of the unfortunate characteristics of this country—to bet on something—anything. You know what Kipling said about Americans?

DAVIS I'm afraid I don't, Mr. Nagel. I majored in civics.

NAGEL "They'll match with destiny for beers." (ED COLLINS *and* BILL CLARK, *detectives, enter*) Come in, gentlemen.

DAVIS Mr. Nagel this is Mr. Collins—and Mr. Clark. Mr. Nagel is president of Custer College.

COLLINS (*Deferentially*) Meeting you is a great pleasure, Mr. President.

NAGEL How do you do, Mr. Collins. Mr. Clark.

CLARK *Gallia est omnis divisa in partis tres.*

NAGEL I beg your pardon?

113

CLARK (*Crossing to the desk*)   *Gallia est omnis divisa in partis tres.*

    (NAGEL *stares at him*)

CLARK I studied Latin in high school.

    (CLARK *sits in the chair left of the desk*)

COLLINS All right, Bill, all right. (*To* NAGEL) I guess the prosecutor has told you why we're here.

NAGEL Yes, gentlemen. This is a pretty serious business.

COLLINS We think so, sir. You see, it fits right into a case our office has been working on for months.

CLARK A national gambling ring, Mr. President.

NAGEL What evidence have you that it involves Custer?

COLLINS Mr. President, all of a sudden, the last two days there's been too much money bet on Ashmore. All around Chicago—

CLARK Cincinnati, Terre Haute, Milwaukee, Las Vegas—

NAGEL I can't follow your line of reasoning from those premises.

CLARK They're all gambling premises.

COLLINS (*Going to the desk*)   I'm a little embarrassed at having to explain anything to a college president, but you must know, sir, that smart money bets smart.

CLARK *Similia similibus percipiuntur.*

NAGEL I see. (*To* DAVIS) Wes, what the hell are they talking about?

TALL STORY

DAVIS   They mean somebody has made sure just how this game is going to come out.

CLARK   That's it. They're the ones we're trying to smoke out.

COLLINS   We thought we might pick up a lead down here. There must be a local contact.

NAGEL   I'm sure it's no one connected with the college.

DAVIS   Of course not, Mr. Nagel, but there's one fellow in town I'm pretty certain makes book—takes bets—although we've never been able to nail him. That's Mike Giardineri.

NAGEL   Giardineri?

DAVIS   Mike—Mike's College Café.

NAGEL   Oh, this is becoming *very* serious. (*To the detectives*) Mike's is the only good restaurant in town.

COLLINS   That's suspicious right there.

NAGEL   Suspicious?

COLLINS   Gamblers like good food.

CLARK   That's right, Mr. President. Big women and good food.

NAGEL   Really? Well, you're never too old to learn.

CLARK   (*Rising*)   Where is this restaurant?

DAVIS   Right across the campus—you'll see the sign.

COLLINS   Come on, Bill. That's where we eat.
(*They cross toward the door*)

DAVIS Boys, I'm glad you're here to handle this. Mike won't spot you. If you get anything on him, take him to my office. Good luck.

COLLINS Great meeting you, Mr. President.
   (CLARK *returns to the desk and shakes* NAGEL's *hand*)

CLARK *Ave atque vale!*
   (*They start out*)

NAGEL I'm curious, what would you expect to find there?

COLLINS We might recognize some of the customers.

CLARK Might hear something—see some money being passed.

COLLINS 'Bye, now.
   (*They exit.* NAGEL, *worried, crosses behind the desk and joins* DAVIS *center*)

NAGEL This affects me very deeply, Wesley.

DAVIS (*Sympathetically*) Yes, Mr. Nagel. I know.

NAGEL Fixed! (*To* DAVIS) I've got fifty dollars bet on Custer!

Black Out

Scene 2

COACH HARDY'S *office. An hour later.*

At rise: RAY *is nervously pacing up and down the right side of the stage, muttering and gesturing. He is not wearing his coat, but is otherwise dressed in his ordinary clothes.* PRESIDENT NAGEL *is holding open one of the double doors leading to the corridor, looking off expectantly. Through this door come the noises of the crowd which is witnessing the basketball game, occasional cheers and frequently the referee's whistle. These are heard each time the doors are opened by anyone coming into or leaving the room. After a moment* NAGEL *comes down to the desk. As the doors close, the sound stops.* NAGEL *picks up the telephone receiver which is off the hook, lying on the desk. As the offstage noise ceases, we hear* RAY *addressing an unseen audience.*

RAY Members of the faculty and fellow students. I want you to listen to me. I've come out here on the floor to tell you why—

NAGEL (*Covering the mouthpiece of the phone with his hand. Irritated*) You're not going out on the floor to tell them anything. Just get that out of your head.

RAY I am if I'm not allowed to play.

NAGEL Young man, we know Mr. Osman and Mr. Solomon are on the way here. They're coming here to give you make-up exams.

TALL STORY

RAY   You've been telling me that for an hour. They're not here yet and the game's started—

NAGEL   You've just got to be patient . . .

RAY   Patient!

NAGEL   (*Into phone*)   Just hold on. I've sent for him.

RAY   Mr. Nagel, I'm even trying to be noble—but I'm getting to the end of my nobility!
   (COACH HARDY *bursts through the door*)

RAY   How's it going?

HARDY   Lousy. (*To* NAGEL) I've called time again. They're not here yet?

NAGEL   You just go on calling time as often as you can. They've got to be here any minute.

HARDY   Mrs. Solomon's here. She's out there watching the game.

NAGEL   She is? Get her in here. She may know where they are.

HARDY   Who've you got on the phone?

NAGEL   Prosecutor Davis's office. They want to talk to him.

HARDY   He's here, too. I saw him.

NAGEL   I know. I've sent for him.
   (*We hear a referee's whistle*)

HARDY   I've got to get out there.
   (*He starts out*)

TALL STORY

RAY Members of the faculty and fellow students, listen to me—

HARDY What's that, Ray?

NAGEL (*To* HARDY) You go ahead—get out there. (HARDY *leaves*) Blent, you've got to stop that. You're just dramatizing this whole thing. I'm not going to—(*He stops short and looks toward the door through which* HARDY *has just left*)—He didn't tell us what the score is.

RAY Oh, we're behind all right. (*He crosses and opens the door. We hear cheering*) That cheering is Ashmore. Mr. Nagel, why can't you give me the examinations? You're the president!

NAGEL It's up to them.
    (JUNE *comes through the door*)

JUNE I've got him.

RAY Good! Which one?

JUNE Mr. Davis.

RAY Davis! We don't want anybody named Davis.
    (*He sinks, dejected, onto the bench, left.* DAVIS *enters*)

NAGEL Here, Wes—(*He hands him the receiver*)—it's your office.

DAVIS Thanks. (*Into telephone*) Hello, Sam. This is Wes.
    (JUNE *has gone over to* RAY)

RAY (*Looking at* JUNE) Members of the faculty and fellow students—I want you to listen to me—

TALL STORY

JUNE It's me, dear, June.
(*She sits beside* RAY)

DAVIS (*Into telephone*) Custer's ten points behind.

RAY That's murder!

DAVIS (*Into phone*) The hell you say! (*Pause*) Where are they? (*Pause*) When did they start? (*Pause*) Will I wait for them? You bet your life I'll wait for them! Thanks, Sam. (*He hangs up and addresses* NAGEL *excitedly*) They've picked up a couple of hoods passing money to Mike Giardineri. Now I've got him. They're bringing them all over here. Now we'll find out who they bribed.

NAGEL Wes, I know who they bribed. Come here a minute.

DAVIS (*Surprised*) You *know!* What's going on around here?

NAGEL (*Taking* DAVIS *to the right side of the room, speaking as he goes*) Wes, remember you said we've got to protect the college—

DAVIS Look, Mr. Nagel, I'm a Custer man—but I'm also an officer of the court. If there's been an arrest—(*They go into a huddle, talking inaudibly for a few seconds.* DAVIS *suddenly speaks with shock*) Blent?

NAGEL Ssh!
(*They continue their huddle in hushed tones*)

JUNE Take it easy, Ray, it's going to be all right. What you said about taking that money—I understand. And you know I love you, don't you? Don't you?

RAY What's the score?

TALL STORY

JUNE   Forty-four to thirty-four. (RAY *groans*) And whatever happens tonight we're going to be married. We're going to be married right away, aren't we?

RAY   How soon will the first half be over?

JUNE   It ought to be over any minute now. Ray, I'm talking about us! Don't you want to talk about us?

RAY   I want you to help me get out there.

JUNE   Why?

RAY   I've got to make a clean breast of everything.

JUNE   Ray, you're the most honorable boy I ever met.

RAY   When the whistle blows at the end of the first half, throw the door wide open. I've got to get out on the floor and tell everybody what I've done.

JUNE   Ray, do you have to be that honorable?

RAY   Open it a crack now, so you can hear.
   (JUNE *goes to the door and opens it a crack. We hear the crowd noises.* RAY *pulls back to be ready to fly through the door.* DAVIS *and* NAGEL *have just about concluded their conference*)

DAVIS   (*Looking at* RAY)   I admire that kid. He's got guts. And I'll tell you one thing, Mr. Nagel, I don't think basketball can take another scandal. This would set Custer back a hundred years.

NAGEL   Well, Wes, not quite that far. Custer was founded only sixty-five years ago.

TALL STORY

(*There is a yell from the crowd and a prolonged blast of the whistle*)

RAY Now! (JUNE *pulls the door open sharply, stepping back as she does. At this moment* MYRA SOLOMON *enters, just in time to collide with the dashing* RAY, MYRA *is knocked to the floor*) Oh, I'm sorry! Excuse me!
(*He starts to pick her up.* NAGEL *takes his arm and throws him to the right side of the stage*)

NAGEL Blent! Get away from that door! Get over there!
(NAGEL *raises* MYRA *to her feet*)

MYRA (*Bewildered*) I think I'm entitled to a free throw.

RAY June, get the coach in here.
(JUNE *exits*)

NAGEL Mrs. Solomon! I'm sorry!
(*He escorts her to the chair below the desk, where he seats her*)

MYRA (*Coming out of the fog and looking around*) Where's my husband?

RAY That's what I want to know. The first half's over.

NAGEL Mrs. Solomon, on the phone you told me your husband and Mr. Osman were on the way down here.

MYRA They started over an hour ago.

RAY Then where are they? They haven't come.

NAGEL What do you think's happened to them?

TALL STORY

MYRA I don't know, Mr. Nagel. (*A sudden thought*) That money! All that money!
 (DETECTIVE COLLINS *sticks his head through the door*)

COLLINS Is Mr. Davis in here?

DAVIS (*Coming around to center*) Here I am.

COLLINS Mr. Davis, I think we've busted this case wide open.
 (OSMAN *strides in angrily, pushing past* COLLINS, *who exits*)

OSMAN (*To* NAGEL) Harmon, you've got to do something about—(*He sees* DAVIS) Wes, this is a hell of a thing to put us through.
 (CLARK *comes into the room, followed by* SOLOMON, *who is handcuffed to him*)

MYRA (*Leaping to her feet*) Leon! What have you done now?

OSMAN (*To* DAVIS) Did you order these men to arrest us?

RAY Professor Solomon, I thought you'd never get here!

SOLOMON (*With hoarse indignation*) Somebody's going to have to answer for this!

DAVIS (*To* CLARK) Get the handcuffs off that man.

RAY Yes! He's got to give me an exam right away.

CLARK Mr. Davis, we caught him passing this bundle of money to Mike.
 (*He holds up the Manila envelope.* DAVIS *takes it*)

DAVIS Get those handcuffs off Professor Solomon!

CLARK He resisted arrest. He took a poke at me.

DAVIS You heard me!
(*Reluctantly,* CLARK *unlocks the handcuffs.* SOLOMON *sits on the bench down left*)

RAY Mr. Osman, can't *you* start? I've got to get in there.
(COLLINS *enters, pushing* MIKE *in ahead of him*)

MIKE What's the idea of putting the arm on me, Mr. Davis? Tell these guys who I am!

COLLINS Shut up, you!

DAVIS He's the one I want to talk to. Take him in there.
(*He points to the inner office.* COLLINS *starts to take* MIKE *there*)

RAY Mr. Davis, will you all clear out of here. I've got to have an exam.

MIKE What's this all about?

COLLINS We'll tell you.
(MIKE *and* COLLINS *exit right*)

CLARK How about this wildcat here. (*He indicates* SOLOMON) He had the money.

DAVIS I'll take care of him. You get in there, too—and wait for me. (CLARK, *bewildered, goes*) Mr. Solomon—Charlie—this shouldn't have happened to you.

SOLOMON It's a little late for apologies.

DAVIS Confidentially, there's been an attempt at bribery.

TALL STORY

OSMAN Wes, we know more about this than you do. That's the money they gave Blent. He got it at Mike's. We were taking it back there, like damn fools.
(The referee's whistle is heard)

RAY That's the second half starting! All this argument's just wasting time—my time.

NAGEL He's right, Wes. Get in there and let them go ahead with the exams.

DAVIS *(Crossing right)* You'd better come with me, Mr. Nagel, I may need you.
(DAVIS *exits into the inner office.* HARDY *bursts into the room, followed by* JUNE)

HARDY Thank God, you're here! Is it all right? Did he pass? Can he go in now?

RAY They haven't even started yet.

NAGEL What's the score, Sandy?

HARDY Fifty-six to forty.

NAGEL Sixteen points—That's a hell of a note.
(He hurries into the inner office)

OSMAN Sixteen points. Let's get to work, Leon. You first.

HARDY Yeah, let's get organized. Ask him something—anything!

RAY Yes, ask me something.
(SOLOMON *deliberately takes time to prepare himself. He rises slowly*)

TALL STORY

SOLOMON Myra, we won't need you.

MYRA Somebody's got to keep score here, too.
(*With pad and pencil from her handbag she sits in the chair below the desk.* SOLOMON *walks very slowly to* MYRA'S *right*)

SOLOMON Blent!
(RAY *draws himself up, prepared to do or die*)

RAY (*Left of desk*) Yes, sir.

SOLOMON Modern ethical theory. Part Two. Second semester.

JUNE (*Taking* RAY'S *hand*) Don't be nervous, Ray. I'm right with you.

HARDY Get in there, kid. We're all with you.

OSMAN Keep out of this, Sandy.
(OSMAN *sits on the bench down left*)

SOLOMON Question Number One: Name the three moralists of the eighteenth century who are representative of traditional ethical theory.

RAY William Paley—Jeremy Bentham—and Immanuel Kant.

SOLOMON Correct.

MYRA One right!

HARDY One right? Three right. He got all three of them.

SOLOMON One right! Question Number Two: How do the basic ethical theories of these men differ?
(RAY *hesitates*)

TALL STORY

HARDY   Toss it right back to him. You can do it.

OSMAN   Shut up, Hardy.
   (*He goes to the outside door and listens. We hear crowd noises. He closes it*)

RAY   (*Haltingly*)   With Paley it was the will of God—with Bentham, the greatest good for the greatest number—with Kant—the idea of what reason demands.

HARDY   (*To* SOLOMON)   Well?

SOLOMON   (*After a pause*)   Well—I'll accept that answer.

MYRA   Two right.

HARDY   I don't know how you guys score. In my book that's six.

SOLOMON   Question Number Three: What modern philosopher may be said to bridge the gap between the skeptics and the existentialists?

RAY   Huh?

HARDY   The exis—what?

RAY   Well, it isn't—
   (*He hesitates*)

JUNE   (*With pretended gaiety*)   It isn't Santa Claus.

RAY   (*Promptly*)   Santayana.

MYRA   Three right.

SOLOMON   Young lady, leave the room!

HARDY   (*To* JUNE)   Yeah—go get Ray's uniform. (JUNE *exits*) Atta boy, Ray, stick in there. You're doing great.

TALL STORY

MYRA   Leon, can't you give him some yes or no's?
(SOLOMON *regards* MYRA *balefully*)

SOLOMON   Question Number Four: How does Ayer's subjectivism differ from traditional subjectivism in relation to ethical judgments of subjective feelings, contrasted with ethical judgments of emotive meanings?

MYRA   That's a yes or no?

OSMAN   Leon, we're sixteen points behind.

RAY *(Sweating)*   Would you please repeat that, sir?

HARDY   We haven't got time to repeat it.

MYRA   I don't think he could anyway.

RAY   I know the answer, but I just don't remember it.

SOLOMON   One wrong.

MYRA *(Sadly)*   Three right. One wrong.

SOLOMON *(Strolling left)*   Question Five: What phrase has Immanuel Kant given to the language of ethics?

RAY *(Promptly)*   The categorical imperative.

SOLOMON   Correct.

MYRA   Four right. One wrong.

HARDY *(Coming to SOLOMON's right)*   That's eighty per cent. That ought to be enough. He's a basketball star. Doesn't he get any points for that?

SOLOMON *(To HARDY)*   I'm warning you—don't interfere.

TALL STORY

HARDY Eighty per cent! What more do you want?

SOLOMON (*Sharply*) I want five more answers!
 (JUNE *runs in with* RAY'*s uniform shirt and shorts, which she gives to the coach*)

JUNE Here's his uniform—

HARDY Ray, get your clothes off.
 (RAY *starts to undress, handing his clothes to* JUNE; *first his shirt*)

SOLOMON Question Six: Explain the categorical imperative.

RAY (*In dismay*) Now?

MYRA Leon, not now.

SOLOMON Now!

RAY Well, it sorta has to do with this (RAY *proceeds with unbuttoning and taking off his shirt*)—that a person can figure out what is right and what is wrong—and rightness makes a demand on you and wrongness doesn't—which means that you ought to do what is right—you're under an obligation to do it—which makes it imperative—and since there can't be any argument about this—that's what makes it categorical and that's why you call it categorical imperative.
 (SOLOMON *hesitates about accepting this, crossing right as he considers it.* RAY *hands his shirt to* JUNE, *receives his uniform shirt and puts it on*)

HARDY O.K. How about it?
 (RAY *hesitates about taking off his pants.* MYRA *goes over between* RAY *and* JUNE, *and turning her back on* RAY,

TALL STORY

spreads out her skirt. RAY *takes off his pants and eventually hands them around her to* JUNE, *as he continues to answer* SOLOMON *over* MYRA'S *shoulder. He receives his basketball shorts in return and hurries into them. In his hurry he puts them on backwards*)

OSMAN   Leon, Kant couldn't have done it any better.

SOLOMON   I'll accept that answer.

HARDY   Atta boy. You're terrific.

MYRA   Five right. One wrong.

SOLOMON   Question Seven: (*He stops to look at* RAY'S *pants*) Aren't your pants on backwards?
   (RAY *looks down at them*)

RAY   Yes, sir.

MYRA   Right! Six right. One wrong.
   (MYRA *again spreads out her skirt as* RAY *hurriedly removes and reverses his shorts*)

SOLOMON   Question Eight: What is the essence of Nietzschean philosophy?

RAY   Well, sir, I never could understand it.

JUNE   Neither could I, Mr. Solomon.

RAY   But I know this much—Nietzsche's wrong.

SOLOMON   And so are you.

MYRA   (*Returning to her chair*)   Six right. Two wrong.

TALL STORY

HARDY   Wait a minute. This is a democracy. He's got a right to his own opinion!

SOLOMON   Question Nine: What philosopher among the ancients most closely parallels the theories of Immanuel Kant?
   (*As he asks this question* SOLOMON *again strolls left*)

RAY   The ancients? Well, that was quite a while ago.

HARDY   Come on, kid—we haven't got much time—

OSMAN   Hardy, for God's sake—quit yelling at the boy—you're making him nervous.
   (JUNE *is mouthing "Socrates"*)

SOLOMON   Answer the question.

HARDY   Take a crack at it, kid. Take a crack at it!?

RAY   (*Tentatively*)   Plato?

SOLOMON   Wrong. It was Socrates.

MYRA   (*Ruefully*)   Six right. Three wrong.

SOLOMON   Blent, you have to get the next one right.

OSMAN   Leon, don't be sadistic! Under these conditions—

SOLOMON   Question Ten—
   (SOLOMON *strolls right, in thought*)

MYRA   Leon—a quickie, huh?
   (HARDY *backs across the stage in front of* SOLOMON)

HARDY   Look, egghead—the kid's only got a few minutes to play. This one's got to be a yes or no. I'm telling you—a yes or no.

SOLOMON   I'll make it a "know." Tell me all you know about Socrates.

OSMAN (*With resignation*)   I give up!
(*He turns and sits down left*)

JUNE   Oh, Mr. Solomon—not all that—

RAY (*Who at the moment couldn't spell cat*)   Well—Socrates was a Greek. He asked people questions and they poisoned him.
(*He directs this defiantly at* SOLOMON)

SOLOMON   Go on! (RAY *stands in empty silence*) I'm waiting! (*Everybody is silently begging* RAY *to talk. He doesn't.* SOLOMON *starts to speak, decisively*) Well, Blent—I'm afraid if that's all you—

OSMAN (*Cutting in*)   Just a minute, Leon. (*Going to* RAY) That answer you gave—is that all you know about Socrates?

RAY (*In despair*)   Yes, sir.

OSMAN   Congratulations! (*He grabs* RAY's *hand and shakes it*) You've passed.

SOLOMON   Wait a minute—

OSMAN   Leon, he answered your question. He told you all he knew about Socrates.
(JUNE *squeals with delight.* MYRA *rises in the excitement.* SOLOMON *sits in her chair in disgust.* HARDY *rushes* RAY *to the door. Then he notices that* RAY *is still in street shoes, socks and garters*)

HARDY Oh, my God! You can't play that way. Where are your shoes?

RAY In my locker.

JUNE I'll get them.
(JUNE *rushes out.* NAGEL *enters from the inner office, followed by* DAVIS, *who is holding the Manila envelope with the four thousand dollars*)

NAGEL What's the score?

MYRA Seven to three.

NAGEL Seven to three?

OSMAN He means the score of the game!

HARDY Oh, my God, there's a game going on!
(*He rushes off.* NAGEL *sees* RAY *in uniform*)

NAGEL Is he going in?

RAY As soon as I can get my right shoes.
(*He now has his street shoes off*)

NAGEL Oh, that's wonderful! (*He goes to* SOLOMON *and claps him on the back*) That's the real Custer spirit. (*He goes to* OSMAN) Charlie, you're a great man.

RAY Where are my shoes?

NAGEL Blent, Custer's counting on you.

BLENT Damn it, Mr. Nagel—go find my shoes!

NAGEL What— Oh—well—yes, of course.
(NAGEL *exits*)

TALL STORY

DAVIS Listen everybody! We've had a great break. They want this whole thing kept off the record. Nothing about this bribery business is to leak out. All of you—just forget it ever happened.

SOLOMON (*Rising and going left*) What I've been through today I'll never forget.

JUNE (*Rushing in with the shoes*) Here you are, Ray!
   (RAY *gets into his shoes and laces them with* JUNE's *help*)

DAVIS We're really getting somewhere. Mike's beginning to talk. We think we can round up the big brass in this syndicate if they don't get suspicious. That's why what's happened here mustn't leak out.

OSMAN Don't worry, Wes, we won't talk.

DAVIS Good! (*He starts out, then suddenly remembers the envelope*) But wait a minute! That puts me on the spot. No one would dare claim this money . . . but I can't hold it. I'd have to enter it on the books. That would make it public. Mike says you gave him this money, Mr. Solomon. (*He puts it in* SOLOMON's *hand*) Remember—I don't know anything about it.
   (*He exits into the office down right*)

SOLOMON This isn't mine. I got it at your house, Charles.
   (*He tries to give it to* OSMAN, *who backs away*)

OSMAN Oh, no, it's not mine.

SOLOMON (*Going to* RAY) Well, Blent, it came from you—

RAY I wouldn't touch it.

JUNE Ray, nobody else wants it.

RAY I never want to see it again.

JUNE Finders keepers.
(*At this moment* RAY *and* JUNE *finish tying* RAY'S *shoes.* HARDY *sticks his head in the door*)

HARDY Blent—where the hell are you?

BLENT Here I come!

SOLOMON (*Blocking his way to the door*) Blent! You haven't passed in physics!

HARDY What?

OSMAN Leon!

SOLOMON Charles!

OSMAN O.K. (OSMAN *crosses to* RAY) Question One: What famous scientist discovered the Einstein theory?
(*The question seems to stump* RAY. *The others are in agony*)

BLENT What? Oh! Einstein!

OSMAN Right. You've passed! Get out there and given them hell.
(*He pushes* RAY *toward the door.* RAY *and* HARDY *rush off*)

JUNE Mr. Osman, I could kiss you for that.
(*She does*)

OSMAN Come on!
(OSMAN *and* JUNE *exit.* SOLOMON *goes up and holds the*

door open, looking off after them. We hear the crowd cheer "Blent! Blent! Blent!" SOLOMON *comes back to center and removes the four thousand dollars from the envelope. Its possession puts him in an unhappy dilemma*)

MYRA Well, Mr. Ethics, here you are with four thousand dollars of somebody else's money. I must say your high principles are beginning to pay off.
(SOLOMON *looks at her*)

Blackout

Scene 3

The SOLOMON *home. After midnight.*
At rise: The stage is dimly lit by the reflection of a light from the head of the stairs. We can see two figures closely intertwined at one end of the couch. The door is opened by MYRA, *who steps in and turns on the lights.* JUNE *jumps off* RAY'S *lap to the left end of the couch.* MYRA, *who is looking out the open door, doesn't see this.* RAY *rises, wiping off his lips.*

MYRA (*Calling out the door*) Do you need any help, Charlie?

OSMAN (*Off*) No, we're fine.
    (*As* MYRA *turns,* JUNE *speaks*)

JUNE Oh, you're back, Mrs. Solomon.

MYRA Sorry we're late. Such a lovely party! President Nagel's! How are the children?
    (*She puts her handbag on the end table and hangs up her coat*)

JUNE Not a peep out of any of them.

RAY Not even Albert.

MYRA I'll take a look at them. (*She waves* RAY *down*) Sit down, Mr. Hero. It's an honor just to have you in our house.
    (*She exits upstairs as* OSMAN *and* SOLOMON *enter. They are wearing their topcoats and hats.* SOLOMON *is obviously a little tight.* OSMAN *steers him over to the couch and seats him between* RAY *and* JUNE)

TALL STORY

SOLOMON Dear Children: I am feeling no pain. Hoping you are the same. Yours truly, Leon Solomon.

JUNE (*Laughing*) Why, Mr. Solomon, that's very cute.
(SOLOMON *is still wearing his topcoat and hat.* OSMAN *removes his own hat and coat and tosses them on the chair down left*)

OSMAN (*Chuckling*) You should have heard him at the party.

SOLOMON (*To* RAY) You were the hero in the game—we were heroes for letting you play in the game. (*Then somewhat wistfully*) I've never been a hero before.

OSMAN (*Going behind the couch*) Leon, to everyone's surprise, including mine, you were a tremendous social success.

SOLOMON Well, I never knew I liked so many people I didn't like.

OSMAN After you, Blent, the most popular man on the campus tonight is Mr. Solomon.

RAY We've always liked you, Professor Solomon.

JUNE Yes, no matter what anybody says.
(MYRA *comes downstairs, stirring something foaming in a glass.* OSMAN *has moved over right*)

SOLOMON (*Puzzled*) Everybody at the party tonight seemed to like me, too. It worries me a little.

OSMAN It worries you?

SOLOMON Have I been true to my principles?

TALL STORY

MYRA I think most of the guests are still there. Would you like to go back and insult them?

SOLOMON I might feel better—but I feel pretty good right now.

MYRA Young lady, you've got a sweet fellow. The night he becomes famous he spends with you, like this.

RAY (*Going to* MYRA) It worked out fine. You see we're driving over to Lakeport a little later.

OSMAN Lakeport?

MYRA Lakeport?

SOLOMON Lakeport! That's where people get married.

JUNE That's right.

RAY There's a fellow over there has to wake up another fellow. (OSMAN *shakes* RAY's *hand*)

JUNE Anybody will do anything for Ray tonight.

RAY Do you mind if we wait for him to call us on the telephone?

MYRA We should have a wedding present for you. But all of ours we've given away.

SOLOMON Yes, we should. After what I put you through tonight—(*To* RAY) I shouldn't have been so hard on you. Halfway through that examination I knew I should have stopped right there—but that coach telling me what I ought to do—(*He pauses*) When my principles are challenged I can be a louse! Yes, we really owe you a fine wedding present.

TALL STORY

MYRA *(Handing him the foaming glass, from behind the couch)* Leon, here's a present for you.
(SOLOMON *drinks it and chokes*)

SOLOMON   You don't serve as good drinks as President Nagel.

OSMAN   You made a big hit with Nagel, Leon. Myra, I'll let you in on a secret . . . Leon's going to be a full professor.

MYRA   He's a full professor now.

RAY   Congratulations, Professor Solomon!

SOLOMON   No, Raymond—if that's your name?

RAY   Yes, sir.

SOLOMON   Tonight the congratulations belong to you.
(SOLOMON *weaves over to* RAY)

RAY   I don't remember much about it, but they tell me I sank twenty-two points.

SOLOMON   I don't mean basketball. That's unimportant. Tonight you won a victory over yourself.

OSMAN   How about you, Leon?

SOLOMON   Maybe I did too. (SOLOMON *manages to reach* OSMAN) Mr. Osman—who is the finest man I have ever known—he said some harsh things to me tonight—and I have a confession to make—(*He hesitates*) I am a little ashamed of this—but confidentially that answer "Santayana" wasn't right. (*He examines his conscience for a moment*) And I have another confession—confidentially, I'm not sorry I accepted it.
(RAY *rejoins* JUNE *on the couch*)

TALL STORY

MYRA Leon, you'd better get to bed. Miss Ryder, how much do I owe you?
   (*She gets her handbag and goes to the left of the couch*)

JUNE It was an hour and a half before dinner and two hours after the game—but take out thirty-five cents for that telephone call to Lakeport.

MYRA That Lakeport call—we'll give you that as a wedding present.
   (*She pays* JUNE, *who puts the money in her handbag, which* RAY *hands to her from the end table*)

SOLOMON Myra, a wedding present has to be more than thirty-five cents.
   (SOLOMON *is at the coat rack, where he hangs up his coat. To do so, he has to take down* JUNE'S *coat. This exchange seems to give him some trouble*)

OSMAN Leon, can you get upstairs all right?

SOLOMON I'll float up.

OSMAN (*To* JUNE *and* RAY, *as he crosses left*) Congratulations again, you two. (*He gets his coat and* MYRA *helps him into it*) You're going to be all right. (*To* JUNE) He's a bright boy and he's got a lot of good jobs waiting for him. (*He picks up his hat*) Sleep tight, Leon.

MYRA How else?
   (OSMAN *goes to the door*)

OSMAN Good night, all.

RAY (*Rising and going to* OSMAN) Mr. Osman, I want to thank you again for being so nice to me tonight and just asking me that one question.

TALL STORY

OSMAN Ray, do you mind if I ask you one more question?

RAY No, sir, go right ahead.

OSMAN (*To* SOLOMON) This is really in your field, Leon. (*To* RAY) Do you know the difference between right and wrong?

RAY (*Soberly*) Yes, Mr. Osman, I think I do now.

SOLOMON And now I'm not sure *I* do.

OSMAN (*After a moment*) I accept both answers.
(*He exits.* MYRA *imparts to* JUNE *an observation she has found to be true, but nonetheless curious*)

MYRA You know, for some reason, with men right and wrong is important.
(*The telephone rings.* RAY *jumps for it*)

RAY I think that's our call. (*Into phone*) Hello... This is Mr. Blent ... I'll hold on ... (*To* JUNE) June, get your coat.

SOLOMON I'll help you on with your coat, Miss Ryder. This is a very special occasion—one I think you will always remember.
(*He helps* JUNE *on with her coat. From one of her pockets peeks a small corner of a Manila envelope*)

RAY (*Into phone*) ... Yeah, Danny, this is me! ... Great! ... We're starting now! (*He hangs up*) They're waiting— good night everybody—(*To* JUNE) I'll start the car—(*He takes his coat from the rack, and speaks to* SOLOMON) Mr. Solomon, you're a swell guy.
(*He rushes out, leaving the door open.* MYRA *holds out her hand to* SOLOMON *who joins her at the foot of the stairs*)

TALL STORY

JUNE   I'll turn out the lights down here.
(*She hurries into the kitchen.* MYRA *and* SOLOMON *start upstairs*)

MYRA   Leon, tonight I admired you.
(*He pats her arm affectionately. They exit up the stairs.* JUNE *comes out of the kitchen and calls up the stairs in a half whisper*)

JUNE   Good night! (*She starts for the door, putting her hands in her coat pockets at the same time. She stops and takes from her pocket the familiar large Manila envelope. From its inside she pulls out a large number of bills. She looks back at the stairs, puts the envelope decisively back into her pocket, jumping up and down in unethical glee. She goes to the outer door and puts her hand on the light switch. She calls out the door*) Ray! Remember my rich aunt that I was telling you about? Well—
(*As she goes out we see her flip the light switch and close the door*)

Curtain